THE SEABEES OF WORLD WAR II

THE SEABEES OF WORLD WAR II

by Commander Edmund L. Castillo, USN

Foreword by Admiral Ben Moreell, CEC, USN (ret.)
Illustrated with official U. S. Navy photographs
Random House   New York

...

Second Edition 2010

2010 Afterword by Christopher Castillo.

This Second Edition designed and arranged by:
Kenneth E. Bingham
Binghamus Press
jorden2323@msn.com

—To Christopher, Who Also Can Do—

THE PHOTOGRAPHS USED IN THIS BOOK are from the files of the U.S. Navy, with the following exceptions: Page 7—Mrs. Robert L. Ryan; page 61—Wide World; page 138—U.S. Marine Corps.

© Copyright, 1963, by Edmund L. Castillo
© Copyright 2010, by the Children of Edmund L. Castillo

All rights reserved under International and Pan-American Copyright Conventions. Published in New York by Random House, Inc., and simultaneously in Toronto, Canada, by Random House of Canada, Limited. Manufactured in the United States of America
Designed by Jerome Kuhl
Library of Congress catalog card number: 63-7828

...

THIS SECOND EDITION IS MADE POSSIBLE
BY
THE CHILDREN OF EDMUND L. CASTILLO
2010

Contents

Acknowledgments		*vii*
Foreword by		
Admiral Ben Moreell, U. S. Navy (Ret.)		*ix*
1.	Welcome Aboard!	3
2.	Bobcats at Borabora	13
3.	"Don't Louse It Up!"	30
4.	Pontoons Bridge the Gap	42
5.	Can Do at Cactus	58
6.	Operation Overlord	80
7.	Conquest of the Marianas	102
8.	The Impossible Takes Longer	116
9.	The Black Sands of Iwo	133
10.	Victory in the Pacific	145
11.	Peacetime Seabees	162
	Bibliography	*185*
	Index	*186*
	Maps Showing:	
	The Pacific Theater	*18-19*
	The European Theater	*52*
	Afterword by Christopher Castillo	*191*

Acknowledgments

This book was begun while Rear Admiral E. J. Peltier was Chief of the Bureau of Yards and Docks, and was completed during the term of Rear Admiral Peter Corradi. Without the assistance of many people in the Bureau, it could not have been written. The author is indebted to Mr. Warren Young, technical information officer; Mrs. Kathryn Zimmerman, historian; Miss Helen R. Fairbanks, formerly historian of the Bureau; and Commander George C. Cornwell. Mrs. Audrey Hanes, director of the Seabee Museum at Port Hueneme, California, also was helpful.

Rear Admiral Paul Blundon, Captain Frank E. Swanson and Mrs. Robert L. Ryan dug into their memories at the author's request and provided facts not recorded elsewhere. Mr. George Baker of the Bureau, Lieutenant Arthur E. Holt of the Navy Office of Information and Mr. Walter V. Barbash of the National Archives helped with pictures. Admiral Ben Moreell read the manuscript and offered several useful suggestions.

The author alone is responsible for any errors or opinions which may have crept into the manuscript, and none of the latter should be attributed officially to the Navy Department.

Foreword

TRYING TO CAPTURE THE SEABEES ON PAPER is a little like trying to describe a wildcat that has the skill of a master mechanic, the tenacity of a bulldog, the speed of lightning, the ingenuity of Thomas Edison, the humor of Bob Hope, and the dedication to duty of John Paul Jones.

The Seabees have all these things, and they have been captured in this, their story for young readers.

The Seabees of World War II tells how the Bobcats, the first unit sent overseas, struggled against unimaginable odds to build a fueling station at faraway Borabora, in the Society Islands of the South Pacific. It describes the gallant, but not very glamorous, battle of the 6th Battalion against the mud of Guadalcanal, and takes the reader to the other side of the globe where Seabees floated two artificial harbors across the English Channel for the invasion of Normandy. Returning to the Pacific, the reader joins sweating Seabee stevedores on the beaches of Guam, catskinners moving earth and coral to build B-29 strips on Tinian and Iwo, and a Seabee reconnaissance party landing in the Philippines only to be surprised by a welcome intended for General MacArthur.

Many of the things the Seabees were told to do had never been done before. This didn't stop them from building cities in the jungle, roads on the sides of mountains, airstrips that leveled hills and bridged valleys, and ice-cream freezers powered by the hot winds of the South Pacific. In a war where nobody was tougher than the United States Marines, the Seabees created a special "Junior Seabee" badge to confer on any Leatherneck who served three months with a Seabee Battalion.

This is not an "official" history of the Seabees, although it was compiled mostly from official sources. It has not been possible in a volume of this size to mention every Seabee unit or even every location where Seabees fought and built. Nor does the author attempt to give individual credit to the hundreds of people in and out of the Navy whose hard work and devotion to their country made it possible to organize the Seabees. I will not do so here. I do want to record my great personal debt to the late Rear Admiral John R. Perry, who, as a commander and later as a captain in the Navy Civil Engineer Corps, was my special assistant in charge of recruiting and training the men who made history as Seabees. His devotion to duty has rarely been equaled and has never been surpassed.

As Chief of the Navy's Civil Engineers throughout World War II, I was proud of my title of "King Bee." I was even more proud of the Seabees themselves, who played such an important part in building the road to victory. The end of the war was not the end of the Seabees, however. They have remained a permanent part of the Navy, and some of the men who built and fought at Normandy, Adak, Guadalcanal and Iwo Jima are still moving earth and pouring concrete for the Navy. Their accomplishments in Korea and their peacetime activities in Japan, the Philippines, Antarctica, the Caribbean, and at home in the United States are related in the last chapter.

I have heard many descriptions of the Seabees. A newspaper man from Arkansas once wrote: "There are all kinds of guys in the Seabees, from the cotton picking champion of Iceland to a former admiral in the Swiss Navy. . . . They can build tank traps with sticks of macaroni, repair a lady's wrist watch with a Stilson wrench, or pitch hay with a one-prong fork. . . ." But I like best General MacArthur's remark to me when I visited him at his headquarters in Australia in 1944:

"The only trouble with your Seabees is that I do not have enough of them."

BEN MOREELL
Admiral, Civil Engineer Corps
U.S. Navy (Retired)
Washington, D.C.

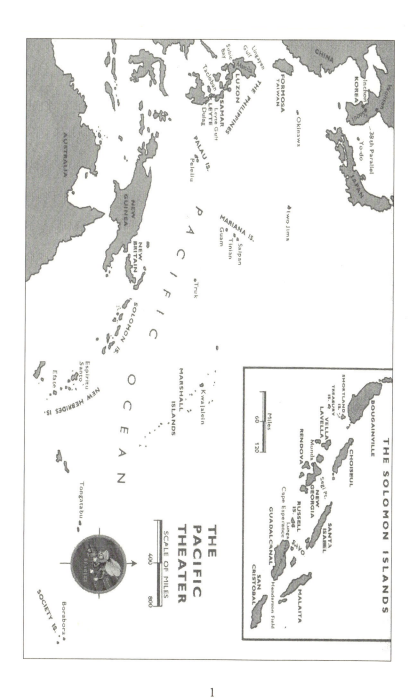

1. WELCOME ABOARD

It was just after midnight when the destroyer slipped away from Russell Island. She was an old ship, a four-stacker left over from World War I and converted for use as a transport. There were faster ships in the Pacific and ships with bigger guns. But this was 1943, and the Navy was glad to have her. The tide was beginning to turn in favor of the United States, and we were going after the Japanese now with any weapons we could get.

The ship's crewmen went about their duties on her darkened decks just as they always did when the little man-of-war went to sea. Sailors stowed mooring lines and walked about checking ports and watertight doors to make sure no crack of light could be seen. Lookouts on the bridge and on the ship's bow peered into the darkness and searched the black sky. Hooded red lights glowed over the compass and the speed indicator on the bridge. The only other light to be seen came from tiny luminous creatures in the water. They glowed for a few seconds, then disappeared, as the ship's passage disturbed the quiet sea.

Near by, a Japanese submarine hunted for targets, fortunately too far away to hear the destroyer's propellers churning the water or the throb of her engines. Occasionally an airplane droned in the distance, a Japanese snooper from Munda flying down to annoy the Marines on Guadalcanal. Gun crews were ready, but the ship's orders were not to fire unless the enemy attacked first. Her mission was a secret one. Its success depended on her reaching the island of New Georgia undetected.

On the bridge with the destroyer's skipper were three men—two Seabees and a Marine. Seabee Commander Bill Painter had landed often on enemy shores. He had come to Russell especially for this mission, a secret reconnaissance of New Georgia, site of the Japanese base at Munda soon to be invaded by the United States Marines. Lieutenant Frank Swanson was less experienced. His outfit, the 47th Naval Construction Battalion, had been picked to go along with the Marines when the time came for the invasion. Now Swanson was going in early with Bill Painter to pick out a site for an airstrip. Then construction could begin on D-day, as soon as the Marines made sure that there were no Japanese on hand to interfere.

The Marine was Lieutenant Colonel Mike Currin, whose small detachment of Raiders were down below, checking their rifles once more and swapping an occasional joke. In a few hours the time for jokes would be past.

Before dawn the destroyer hove to off Segi Point, the southern tip of New Georgia. A seaman on the bridge flashed a carefully shielded light toward the shore. If all went well, there would be an answering flash. If not, the next flash might come from Japanese guns.

Seconds ticked by. Then far across the water a light blinked briefly on the shore. Mike Currin ordered his Marines to the ship's rail. Silently, destroyer men lowered a boat into the water. Currin and his Marines slipped over the side and were gone. A second boat was lowered for the Seabees, and soon it, too, was headed for the beach.

The sun was still below the horizon when the first boat touched the beach at Segi Point, but the sky had changed from inky black to transparent blue. Now it was possible to see the outlines of the jungle and some hills beyond. The light on the shore had flashed briefly several times to guide the incoming boats, but now the beach seemed deserted. The Marines leaped ashore ready for trouble. The signals could be a trap. With Colonel Currin in the lead, they cautiously advanced.

Suddenly something stirred in the jungle. Bushes parted and out stepped a single figure in green fatigues. The Marines, fingers on their triggers, found it hard to hold their fire. There was a moment of silence. Then the man in green stepped forward and spoke:

"Colonel, the Seabees are always happy to welcome the Marines to enemy territory!"

The man in green was Seabee Lieutenant Bob Ryan, a 49-year-old California engineer. Ryan had fought in the Army during World War I and joined the Navy in 1942. He had landed on Segi Point nine days earlier with two Army officers. They had been playing hide-and-go-seek with the Japanese army ever since.

Ryan and his two companions also had come to Segi in a destroyer. In their case, the signals on the shore had come from natives, members of a private "army" organized by Donald Kennedy, a New Zealander who lived on an abandoned plantation near by. Kennedy had been a district officer in the island government before the war. Now he lived alone in the jungle. Secretly, he kept in touch by radio with British and American forces, warning them of Japanese movements and arranging for the rescue of downed fliers. Ryan's party had been paddled ashore in a dugout canoe by Kennedy's natives, who worked against the Japanese at night and melted into the jungle by day.

There were other small reconnaissance parties on the island, too. Their orders were to remain in small groups. This would help them stay hidden, and might insure that some

Welcome Aboard

Robert L. Ryan (left) and one of the Pacific Island natives who helped him hide out from the Japanese.

would survive in case others were caught by the Japanese.

Aided by the natives, Ryan and the two Army officers scouted the tangled jungle and surveyed the landing beaches. They had brought a rubber landing boat ashore. They kept it hidden in the dense underbrush, but when the coast was clear they could inflate it and paddle about making soundings with a bamboo pole or a weighted line. In this way they located coral reefs that could cause trouble for landing craft. They also measured the rise and fall of the tides along the beaches.

Ryan's group was joined after a day or two by another three-man party. The six men worked together during most of their stay on the island. Natives helped them a great deal, warning them of Japanese patrols and leading them to safe camp sites. Once they took Ryan to a spot where an American aviator lay wounded after having been shot down over the enemy island. Risking the use of their radio, Ryan and his companions arranged to have him picked up by a destroyer at night. In the darkness they carried him to the shore, and natives quickly spirited him away in a canoe to meet the ship.

Another night the six-man party came upon a group of Japanese soldiers camped about a small fire. Creeping forward, the Americans quietly brought their heavy, water-cooled machine gun within range. Then as one man fired the gun, the others hurled grenades into the Japanese camp. Later they found eleven dead Japanese soldiers in the camp.

It was after this adventure that the Marine Raiders were sent to Segi as reinforcements, while Bill Painter's small group went in to finish surveying the island. A few nights later, Ryan's group climbed into native canoes and silently slipped away to a waiting destroyer. Their part of the job was done.

Bill Painter's party stayed at Segi, carrying on the survey. And in less than a week Ryan was back on the island. This time his landing wasn't secret. The Marines were landing in force, and along with them came most of the 47th Construction Battalion, including Lieutenant Bob Ryan. Their LST (landing ship, tank) hit the beach at 10:10 the morning of June 30, 1943. The Seabees had their construction equipment unloaded and had begun work on the airstrip by 3:00 that afternoon. Nine days later, the first plane landed where before there had been a wild jungle. By the eleventh day a whole squadron of fighters was operating from the Segi strip. Now American bombers flying from Guadalcanal to attack Munda, only forty miles from Segi Point, would have fighter cover as they approached the enemy base.

The Seabees had worked around the clock to build that strip. At night they worked by searchlight, turning the lights off when Japanese bombers attacked.

It rained most of the time, more than fourteen inches

A Navy SBD "Dauntless" dive bomber flies over the Segi Point airstrip on New Georgia Island.

during those eleven days, by official count.

Bill Painter soon went on to new jungles. His name was to become a legend in the Pacific. Meanwhile, Bob Ryan was promoted and became executive officer of the 47th Battalion. A few months later he received a letter of commendation from Admiral William F. Halsey, commander of the South Pacific Area, for his work on Segi. Then in January, 1944, on his fiftieth birthday, he was awarded the Legion of Merit by the United States Army. The citation read, in part, "Lt. Cdr. Ryan's superior professional skill, tireless energy and enthusiasm were largely responsible for the construction so necessary to the United States Armed Forces in their drive on the enemy."

This was a big day for Bob Ryan, but no bigger than the day back at Segi when a jeep came tearing down the dusty road and skidded to a halt where Ryan was standing near the airstrip. Out jumped a salty little character in khaki with the four stars of an admiral on his collar.

"Halsey's the name," he said, sticking out his hand. "I heard you Seabees built this airstrip in nine days and I couldn't believe it, so I've come to see for myself!"

Halsey saw and believed. Later, after visiting another Pacific island, he told a radio audience that the Seabees were clearing a field, "and I had to run most of the time to keep from being shoveled into the ocean."

The Seabees never did shovel an admiral into the sea, but

if they had been told to do so there is no doubt what their answer would have been:

"CAN DO!"

2. BOBCATS AT BORABORA

The United States entered World War II only half prepared to fight a major war and not really convinced that its enemies were very tough. American newspapers and newsreels had been making fun of the Germans, Japanese and Italians for months. Hitler was pictured as a ridiculous little man with mussy hair and a postage-stamp mustache; Mussolini was a fat, bald show-off with a big lower lip and puffed-out cheeks. And everyone was confident that Americans were superior to the short, spectacled Japanese, who lived on crowded islands far across the Pacific and were best known in the United States for cheap imitations of American products.

Suddenly Pearl Harbor changed all that. The Japanese caught America napping. They sank much of the mighty United States Pacific Fleet in the harbor and destroyed

Army Air Corps planes at Hawaii's Hickam Field. American garrisons at Guam and Wake were battered into submission. In a few short weeks, the United States lost control of the Central Pacific and was forced to retreat from the Philippines. Japanese forces drove into Southeast Asia and threatened Australia and New Zealand.

On the other side of the world, German submarines were sinking American ships carrying men and supplies to Britain. France had fallen and the Allies had lost their foothold on the mainland of Europe. German planes were bombing London practically every night. The Allied position had become desperate.

In Washington, high-ranking Army and Navy officers were trying to map out strategy to retrieve Allied losses and win the war. First they must stem the tide of the advancing Japanese in the Pacific. Then they would give all possible aid to England, free France, and defeat Germany and Italy on the continent of Europe. When victory had been won there, the Allies would turn their full strength against the enemy in the Pacific.

It was a good plan. All it required was a bigger and better Army than the United States and Britain had, more bombers than anyone had ever dreamed of, a two-ocean navy, supply ships and more supply ships, and bases overseas.

Bases were important. Planes flying from America to Europe needed fuel stops at places such as Iceland and the

Bobcats at BoraBora

The USS Arizona, a victim of the Japanese surprise attack at Pearl Harbor, lies wrecked in the mud.

Azores. Ships and planes patrolling the Atlantic and Pacific in search of enemy submarines could operate farther from home shores if they had bases in Bermuda, the Caribbean, Midway and the Aleutians. The Allies would need bases in England and North Africa to invade Europe. And the only way to beat Japan would be to gain control of the Pacific, island by island, moving westward in a long series of amphibious assaults. Bases would be the key to victory. Without them, the Allies could not win the war.

In peacetime, base construction had been a job for civilians. The Army or Navy told a civilian contractor what was wanted, and the contractor hired engineers and construction workers to do the job. But civilians had no business overseas once the war began. They weren't trained to fight, and even the most patriotic construction workers were not eager to go unarmed where they might be attacked or captured without even a chance to fight back. And if they did fight—as any red-blooded American certainly would—they might be executed immediately as guerrillas if the enemy captured them. So the Army and Navy had to figure out ways to do the job themselves —along with all the other jobs that had to be done if the war was to be won.

The man the Navy turned to was Rear Admiral Ben Moreell (pronounced More-ELL), Chief of the Bureau of Yards and Docks. As the boss of all the Navy's civil engineers, he had the job of supervising the building and maintenance of bases wherever the Navy might need them.

Admiral Moreell had seen the problem coming his way. About five weeks before the Japanese had attacked, he had begun to organize a few units of Civil Engineer Corps officers and skilled petty officers who could take over construction jobs overseas if war were to break out. When the war began, he expanded this idea. He proposed that the Navy recruit the country's best builders and engineers, put them in uniform, and send them out to build whatever was needed. Let them move hills, fill valleys, make roads, change the course of rivers, build harbors, pave airstrips in the jungle, build anything anywhere. And teach them how to fight the enemy in their spare time.

The Navy liked the idea. On January 5, 1942, less than a month after Pearl Harbor, Admiral Moreell's superiors told him to begin recruiting the men who were to form the Navy's Construction Battalions. These were the men who were to be known around the world as the Seabees.

The first Navy construction unit was formed at Newport, Rhode Island, and trained for duty in Iceland. But before the outfit was ready to sail, its destination was changed from north to south and from east to west. For as the Japanese took over more and more of the Pacific, Admiral Ernest J. King, Commander in Chief of the United States Fleet, found that he needed a fueling station for ships carrying supplies to Australia and New Zealand. The site of the sta-

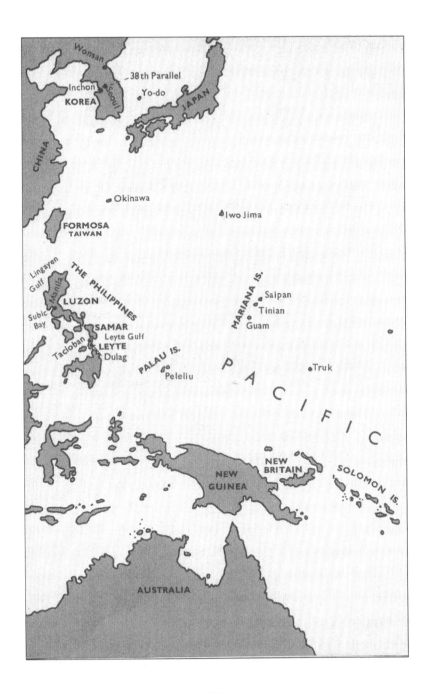

Bobcats at BoraBora

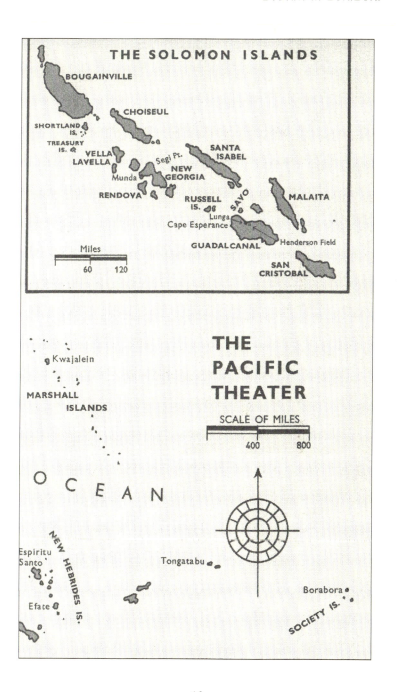

tion was to be the tiny, tropical island of Borabora, more Than 2,000 miles south of Hawaii.

Building the base would take about 300 Navy construction men. To the 99 partly trained men at Newport, Moreell added 7 newly commissioned Naval Reserve officers, a few cooks and gunner's mates, and about 140 new recruits fresh from "boot camp." Lieutenant Commander Harold McTavish Sylvester, a Civil Engineer Corps officer in the Regular Navy, was placed in charge, and the unit was ordered to sail.

Plans had to be kept secret, so the men were told only that they were headed for a place that went by the code name "Bobcat." It wasn't long before they began calling themselves the Bobcat Detachment, a name that was to stick with them for the rest of the war.

There was some construction equipment at Newport, and it was loaded aboard ship with the Bobcats. Then the unit sailed to Norfolk, Virginia, to pick up more equipment. At Charleston, South Carolina, the Bobcats were joined by about 4,000 Army troops who were to defend the island of Borabora and its vital fuel depot from Japanese attack.

Plans called for "combat loading" the ships so that the items needed first would be on top where they could be unloaded quickly. But the Army and Navy were inexperienced in combat loading. Construction equipment that came aboard at Newport and Norfolk went to the bottom of the ships' holds. A lot of less important equipment was loaded on top at Charleston.

There were other mix-ups, too. Guns that were to be mounted on the deck of one of the transports for self-defense accidentally were loaded below with the cargo. To get them out again, the Seabees had to unload a carload of lumber and fifty tons of other material. Another ship was so top-heavy after her guns were mounted that the Bobcats had to mix a batch of heavy concrete—cement, sand, gravel and scrap metal—and ballast her with 1,500 tons of the stuff before the convoy could sail. But sail it did, on January 27, 1942, only two days behind schedule and exactly a month after Admiral King had ordered the Borabora expedition organized.

A month later, the Bobcats saw their new home. After the cramped life aboard ship, any land would have looked good. But now they were looking at a real tropical paradise. First it was just a speck on the horizon. Then the island's high twin peaks, Temanu and Pahia, came clearly into view, seeming to change from a dull gray against the horizon to a bright green as the convoy approached. The water, such a brilliant blue in the South Pacific, turned lighter and shaded into green toward land. Then it burst into a dazzling white as the breakers rolled across the coral reef surrounding the island.

The ships steamed slowly through the passage in the reef into a sheltered harbor. One by one they dropped anchor. Soldiers and sailors crowded the rails to stare at the little town of Vaitape with its government buildings flying the French flag, native huts with palm-thatched roofs, and the single pier so inadequate for the task of unloading the convoy.

Ashore, most of the island's 1,400 inhabitants stared back in friendly amazement.

Commander Sylvester and his officers looked at their charts, based on a nineteenth century survey, and began to realize—if they hadn't before—the size and difficulty of the task before them.

Sylvester went ashore immediately, along with the Army general who was to command the island. First they flew over the island in a small seaplane, looking for the best spots to build the tank farm and airstrip. Then they walked about the island to get a closer look. When they returned, the ships started to unload.

The trouble began right away. The pier at Vaitape was much too small for the transports to tie up alongside. In fact it couldn't even accommodate heavy equipment brought ashore in barges. So one of the Bobcats' first assignments was to cut two wide trenches leading from the harbor back into a level stretch of solid ground. Barges carrying heavy equipment could then be piloted into these artificial bays and unloaded directly onto the island.

Unloading was no simple task. It was fairly easy to transfer cargo from the ships onto barges, because the ships' own deck booms could be used. But once the barges came in to the beach, they had to be unloaded by hand. There were no

Bobcats at BoraBora

Bobcat officers pore over construction plans in an improvised open-air office on Borabora.

Since Borabora had no modern harbor facilities, the Bobcats had to unload cargo by hand.

cranes on the island, and the Bobcats' own cranes were at the bottom of one of the ships' holds. It took three weeks for the Bobcats to find a crane, get it onto the beach, and set it up where it could unload the barges. Tractors and trucks also were on the bottom of the holds. A lot of low-priority equipment had to be brought ashore and spread out over a two-mile stretch of beach before the Bobcats could unload trucks to haul it away.

The Army troops moved ashore as soon as possible, taking along their tents, which had been packed on top of the Bobcats' construction equipment. Gradually the Bobcats dug down to find the frames and sheet steel to build their own Quonset huts. These were long, narrow huts with domed roofs, named for Quonset, Rhode Island, where they were first used. Within three weeks, the Bobcats had erected 400 of the huts ashore. By that time eight galleys—Navy lingo for mess halls—were set up and operating on the island.

More problems developed during the six weeks it took to finish unloading the ships. The island's water supply was inadequate, and the Bobcats had to build four dams and a thirteen-mile pipe line before they could do very much else. There was only one major road on the island, a two-lane affair made of coral and sea shells. The Army's big trucks weighed several tons unloaded, and they soon broke down most of the island's bridges and reduced the road to a sea of mud. Finally the huge vehicles had to be banned from use until the Bobcats could build a better road.

Nearly three months passed before the Bobcats could begin work on the fuel depot they had been sent to Borabora to build. They and the Army troops fought the weather, the insects, the mud and the jungle just to survive—and there were times when they nearly fought each other. Commander Sylvester later reported that during those first few months the Bobcats "smelled like goats, lived like dogs, and worked like horses."

Finally on May 1, Admiral Chester Nimitz, Commander in Chief of the Pacific Fleet, sent Commander Sylvester a personal radio message. Tankers were coming soon, carrying fuel for the Borabora depot. When would Bobcat Base be ready to receive them? Sylvester hesitated a moment, then radioed back that the storage tanks would be built by June 15, only six weeks away. The Army general was skeptical but, when he saw that Sylvester had already answered the Admiral, he made Army troops available to help build the tank farm. Six weeks later the tankers arrived. The Bobcats up in the hills were still tightening bolts on some of the tanks as fuel began to flow up the pipe line from the beach.

The Bobcats built an airfield on Moto Mute, a nearby island that was scarcely more than a wide spot in the coral reef. And they constructed a seaplane base with hangars and a ramp to bring the big planes up onto dry land. They built eleven miles of road, two radio stations, a pier and

Bobcats at BoraBora

At Borabora the Bobcats built this pier (above) to unload the huge guns which the Army expected to need for island defense. The gun barrel rests in a specially built wooden sled that rides on rollers made from lengths of pipe. Once ashore, the guns had to be hauled up a steep hill (below) to the emplacements the Bobcats had built for them. A gasoline-powered winch did some of the pulling, but the Bobcats had to guide the thirteen-ton barrels.

a dry dock. Perhaps the hardest job—more difficult even than building the fuel depot—was mounting guns they had brought along to defend the island. Each gun barrel weighed about thirteen tons—as much as six or seven automobiles. They had to be dragged by hand to their emplacements almost half a mile up steep hills. The breech blocks and gun mounts weighed about as much as the barrels, and they, too, had to be moved by hand. In all, the Bobcats mounted eight of the big guns in the Borabora hills. As fate would have it, none of them ever was fired at a Japanese ship. Although the island was bombed a few times, the Japanese never attacked Borabora from the sea.

A lot of mistakes were made on Borabora, but many worse errors had been made before the convoy ever left the United States. Wheelbarrows were shipped without wheels. The Bobcats were furnished the wrong kind of trucks and they didn't have enough spare parts to keep them running. There weren't enough hand shovels to go around. They had welding equipment but no welders' masks, blacksmiths' forges but no coke for the fires, not enough screens for their Quonset huts, and not even enough nails. But this was the first advance base the Navy built under combat conditions, with construction forces, occupation troops, and base equipment all arriving the same day in a single convoy. The Navy learned a great deal at Borabora, enough so that the same mistakes in planning, training, loading and unloading never were made again. The lessons the Bobcats learned the hard way resulted in the better preparation of the battalions that followed them into the Pacific.

It was a good deal later in the war that the Seabees picked up their unofficial motto, "Can do!" But no gang of Navy construction men ever was called on to do more in less time, with less equipment and less help, than the Bobcats were expected to accomplish at Borabora.

3. Don't Louse It Up!

While the Bobcats were blasting tank sites out of solid rock and hauling steel plates ashore with their bare hands, the Navy was working seven days a week organizing and training more construction units. There had been one such outfit at Great Lakes Naval Training Station during World War I, but it was organized late in the war. Its mission was to do construction work at the Training Center. Except for a small detachment that went to France, these construction men did not serve overseas. This time the Navy was getting an earlier start. Admiral Moreell could see that World War II was going to be a long war. It would cover two oceans and more islands than most Americans knew existed. Navy construction men were going to be needed in great numbers, and it was his job to get them.

Don't Louse it Up

The Admiral sent recruiting teams to construction firms and labor unions. Experienced construction engineers were given commissions in the Navy's Civil Engineer Corps. Construction workers of all types were recruited as enlisted men. There were steel workers and carpenters, builders and electricians, surveyors, plumbers and truck drivers, tractor operators and draftsmen, machinery repairmen, riggers, lumberjacks, demolition men and many others. Just as the more experienced engineers were appointed to the higher ranks, construction workers with many years on the job—especially those who had supervised large groups—were given petty officer ratings.

Most of these men already were skilled in their trades, so the Navy didn't have to train them in the duties of their ratings as it did other sailors. But it did have to teach them some Navy discipline. And they had to know enough about jungle warfare to be able to defend themselves as well as build bases. For they were going to do their building in some dangerous spots. More than once they found themselves grading or paving one end of an airstrip while the Marines were fighting the enemy at the other. At Bougainville in the South Pacific, for instance, one "can do" road-building outfit got 700 feet ahead of the front lines and had to wait for the rest of the war to catch up.

The first training camps were at Quonset Point and Norfolk. Later one was opened at Port Hueneme (pronounced

Wy-NEE-mee by the Seabees) in California. The camp at Quonset Point became the Naval Construction Battalion Training Center, Davisville, Rhode Island. It and Hueneme are the Seabees' two chief bases today.

Teaching military discipline to a gang of construction workers was something of a problem. They got the "can do" idea right away, but the niceties of naval etiquette just never rubbed off on some of them. Throughout the war, the Seabees remained a good deal more informal than the seagoing Navy. The Seabees tell the story—although they insist it isn't typical—of a sentry standing his watch at night in one of their camps in North Africa.

"Who are you?" he challenged, as a shape appeared in the darkness.

"A friend," came the answer.

"Well, if you're a friend, what the heck are you doing over there?" said the Seabee. "Come on over here."

"Son," asked the stranger, "do you know who I am?"

"No, who?"

"I'm the Admiral in charge of this operation."

The Seabee was impressed. "Whaddya know? In charge of the whole shebang?"

"Yes, in charge of the whole shebang."

"Well," said the Seabee, "it's a pretty good job, Bub, "Don't louse it up!"

Don't Louse it Up

Before going overseas, expert construction men learn how to handle a new tool at a training-camp rifle range.

It was at Quonset Point that the construction men got their name and insignia. The name "Seabee" grew from the initials "C.B." for "Construction Battalion." Frank Lafrate, Carpenter's Mate, First Class, stationed at Quonset, designed the Seabees' insignia, a furious, fighting bee wearing a sailor's hat and carrying a hammer, a wrench, and a Tommy gun. The name and insignia were officially approved by the Navy Department in March, 1942.

The 1st Naval Construction Battalion was commissioned that same month and shipped out for "Bleacher" and "Roses," the islands of Tongatabu and Efate several hundred miles west of Borabora. The 2nd Battalion was commissioned a month later, and it, too, headed for the South Pacific. By June, the Navy had nine Seabee battalions, in addition to the Bobcat Detachment, and by early summer Seabees were serving in the South and Central Pacific, Alaska, and Iceland.

A battalion was made up of about thirty officers and more than a thousand men. It was led by a commander or lieutenant commander in the Civil Engineer Corps and was divided into four construction companies, each under a lieutenant. The officer second in command of the battalion, usually a lieutenant or lieutenant commander, was the executive officer. Each battalion also had its own medical and dental officers, supply officers, and a chaplain. Cooks, storekeepers, and a few other non-construction ratings made up a small

At Port Hueneme, California, members of a Naval Construction Battalion board a transport bound for the Pacific.

headquarters company. When several battalions were assigned to a single area, they usually were organized into construction regiments, each consisting of several battalions. For very large operations, they were combined into construction brigades, each of which contained two or more regiments.

Seabee training, planning and equipment were designed to solve the problems that the Bobcats had to whip the hard way at Borabora. As a result, the Seabees that went into the Pacific and north to Iceland in 1942 were ready for just about anything. If they needed something they hadn't brought with them, they built it. If they couldn't build it, they managed to "borrow" it from the Army, or from the Japanese. While the Army washed its socks in its helmet liners, the Seabees were building windmill-powered washing machines in the Aleutians and throughout the Pacific. When the Bobcats couldn't find insulators, they strung their electric wires on Coca-Cola bottles. When they had no electric sockets, they made their own out of tin cans. Other Seabees made drainage pipes, ice-cream freezers, and roofing out of empty oil drums, and engine gaskets out of letters from home.

At one island the Seabees set up an electric power system using equipment from nine different countries. To a Swiss engine that happened to be on the island they hooked up a generator the Japanese had left behind. They used transformers

Don't Louse it Up

A Seabee on a Pacific island loads his "cumshaw" washing machine. The clothes go into the drum, which is then placed on the plank under the tower. As the windmill spins, the plunger—an inverted funnel—goes up and down to slosh the clothes about in the water.

from France, New Zealand and the United States, and wired the system with Italian cable. The heavy equipment was mounted in concrete made with Australian cement. A German gadget oiled the moving parts, and heavy lifting was done with a Dutch chain hoist. The Seabees kept this outlandish rig going for a year. In all that time, the power was out for a total of only six hours and ten minutes.

The Navy uses the word "cumshaw" to describe any supplies or services obtained without a properly signed requisition. The Seabees are recognized throughout the Navy as its champion "cumshaw artists." One Seabee who helped build that reputation was Warrant Officer Robert C. Straub of the 15th Battalion. Bob Straub had sold machinery on the West Coast of the United States before he joined the Seabees. Some of his customers had been as far away as New Zealand. So he took matters into his own hands when his outfit found itself on the island of Espiritu Santo in the South Pacific with a large amount of repair work and no machine shop.

First he wangled an airplane ride to New Zealand, where he got in touch with some of his old customers. Sure enough, they were having difficulty getting materials because of the war, and some of the machinery he had sold them was standing idle. Straub talked a Navy supply officer into buying the equipment and got permission from the New Zealand government to take it out of the country. Then he arranged for some cumshaw transportation back to his outfit in the war zone. There he set up a complete machine shop that soon was serving not only the Seabees but the seagoing Navy, the Army, the Air Corps and the Marines as well. Whenever he could, he would swap a little extra repair work for a lathe, a drill press, or some other piece of machinery some other outfit didn't need. Before long, the 15th had the best equipped shop in the whole Pacific!

Another South Pacific outfit showed its ingenuity, and incidentally saved several valuable working days, when it was ordered to move two tall water tanks across an island from the port where they had been delivered by a ship. The tanks were thirty-two feet tall. Since the only road led through a town where the telephone wires were strung only fifteen feet above the ground, the island commander told the Seabees to take the tanks apart, move them in sections, and put them together at the other end of the line. Seabee Lieutenant Commander Robert Arthur had other ideas, however. That night he mustered a group of his electricians and loaded the tanks on two lowboy trailers. Half the electricians climbed on the first truck and the other half rode the second. As the town slept, the strange procession made its way slowly across the island. Whenever they came to a telephone wire, the Seabee electricians quietly snipped it with wire cutters. Then as the second tank passed the spot, they spliced the lines together again. The tanks were delivered before dawn, and no one was ever the wiser, although Bob Arthur admits that there may have been a few wrong numbers on the island for a few days.

One of the toughest jobs at every island base was unloading supplies and equipment from ships and landing craft without the aid of piers. At one island the Seabees actually built three artificial beaches for amphibious vehicles by pouring more than a thousand truckloads of crushed coral into the lagoon between the island itself and the coral reef that surrounded it. This job, of course, was done after the island had been secured by our own forces.

At Vella Lavella in the Solomons, however, one man did almost as well under combat conditions. The Seabees landed at Vella Lavella with the assault force. They were having a hard time getting their equipment ashore, for the landing craft were grounding on a reef some distance off the beach. The water was too shallow for the boats to cross the reef, but it was too deep for the tractors to drive through. Chief Yeoman Herb Minster, who had been a lumberjack in Idaho before he joined the Navy, gathered up a crew of his Seabee mates and splashed ashore with axes and rope. In a short time they had cut down enough palm trees to bridge the distance between the landing craft and the beach. Then they drove the first bulldozer ashore. The rest of the job was simple. The bulldozer just scooped up enough coral and sand to make a solid causeway over the palm logs, and the Seabees were able to drive their equipment in to the beach without getting their wheels wet.

Herb Minster's job as a yeoman was to take care of the battalion's paper work. He had no business out there cutting down trees and directing a work gang. But Minster was a Seabee, and Seabees can do anything—especially under enemy fire.

4
Pontoons Bridge The Gap

While Herb Minster was felling palm trees at Vella Lavella, the Navy's Bureau of Yards and Docks in Washington was working on a better way to bridge the gap from ship to shore. For some months, a Civil Engineer Corps captain named John Laycock had been gluing cigar boxes together with kite sticks. His boxes went a long way toward winning the war.

Laycock got the idea from a report written by another Navy civil engineer in 1936. That officer had suggested that large steel pontoons could be bolted together to form barges for use at advance bases. The barges could be made in any size or shape needed. If one or two pontoons were damaged by collision or gunfire, the remaining cells would provide enough buoyancy to keep the barge afloat. The Bureau of

Yards and Docks had studied the idea, worked out some more details, and then filed the papers away in its war-plans safe. About two years before the Japanese attacked Pearl Harbor, Captain Laycock ran across the file.

The idea looked like a good one, and Laycock soon was experimenting with models of cigar boxes, testing arrangements of different sizes and shapes for strength and stability. By the fall of 1940, he had worked out most of the details for a standard pontoon and the hardware—later nicknamed "jewelry"—to connect the pontoons together. In May, 1941, the first pontoons were delivered to the Navy for testing.

Laycock's pontoons were made of heavy steel and measured five by seven by five feet. Empty, one weighed about a ton and would float in about a foot and a half of water. The top of the pontoon, not much bigger than the top of an ordinary double bed, was designed to support twenty tons. This is about the weight of a family of African elephants—father, mother and baby—or five full-grown hippos.

Steel beams were bolted along the top and bottom corners to connect the pontoons into strings, just as the kite sticks had been glued to the edges of Captain Laycock's cigar-box models. In the first test of the pontoons, a string of eleven was suspended between two supports to form a bridge. Then steel plates were piled in the center of the span to see how much weight it could hold. One of the steel beams finally gave way when the load reached fifty-five tons,

Captain Laycock (right) invites Admiral Moreell to lean on a cigar-box model of a string of pontoons.

Pontoons Bridge The Gap

The Seabees took only a few hours to build this ten-by-four pontoon pier for unloading small craft.

the equivalent of eight elephants and their keepers.

The Seabees found that the pontoons had many uses. Two strings of six or eight boxes each, bolted side by side, made a perfect causeway for unloading heavy equipment from landing craft. A pier could be built in a hurry by bolting together two or three strings of the desired length, anchoring one end to the beach with wire cable, and securing the other end to pilings driven into the bottom of the harbor. A couple of short strings could be placed across the end of the pier like the crossbar on the letter "T" to make a small wharf.

To make a stronger wharf that could handle large barges or even cargo ships, the Seabees started by sinking a string of pontoons in about a foot or two of water parallel to the beach. Then they filled the space between the pontoons and the beach with sand and coral. The next step was to place several pier sections at right angles against the sunken string, one end anchored to it, the other jutting out into the stream. Finally another long section two or three strings wide was secured across the outboard ends of these piers. The result was a floating wharf out in deep water, parallel to the beach and connected to it by several causeways wide enough and strong enough to carry heavy equipment ashore.

A barge that could carry fifty tons of cargo—approximately the weight of twenty-five large automobiles—was made by bolting together, side by side, three strings of seven pontoons each. A one-hundred-ton barge was made of four strings, each string being twelve pontoons long. For really big loads, six strings of eighteen boxes each were used to form a barge more than one hundred feet long and forty feet wide. It could carry 250 tons of supplies or equipment.

To move the barges, the Navy ordered the world's biggest outboard motors. Approximately the size of a large tractor engine, one motor and operator's station took up most of one pontoon. Another type of propulsion unit had the engine mounted inside the pontoon.

The Seabees used Captain Laycock's boxes for much more than just carrying cargo. A small barge, made up of two strings of seven pontoons each, was used in the Aleutian Islands as an icebreaker. It could pound its way through ice up to a foot thick. A gate vessel, used for opening and closing the entrance to the anti-submarine net at a harbor entrance, was made by mounting a search light, a gasoline winch and a small hut on a four-by-twelve barge. Three big fuel tanks on a six-by-eighteen barge made a fine filling station for small craft.

Other important barge rigs were tug boats, dredges, pile drivers and floating cranes. Tugs were made of two short strings and one long one—with motors mounted on the two outboard strings. They were used to handle larger barges and even ships. A warping tug was made by mounting a power winch on a 7-12-7 tug barge. Using a 9,000-pound anchor to hold itself stationary, it could pull a load of more than 50,000 pounds. It was particularly useful when a ship or large barge had to be turned in a small space such as a river mouth or a small harbor.

In all, more than thirty standard barge assemblies were used, and a good many others were invented on the spot by Seabees who needed something special in a hurry.

One of the most ingenious uses for the pontoons was in the construction of floating dry docks to lift damaged craft out of the water for repairs. The floor and sides of these docks were made of pontoons. Pipes and valves were added so that the floor pontoons could be flooded with sea water to make the dock sink. Set in about twenty feet of water, the dock would settle to the bottom with its sides above the surface. While the dock was in this position, a damaged PT boat or other small craft would be floated into the dock. Then the Seabees would pump compressed air into the pontoons. The air would force the water out of the pontoons, and the dock would gradually rise until its deck was above the surface. That would lift the damaged boat high and dry, where a repair crew could work on it. The same principle was used in a seaplane dock which the Seabees invented to lift the Navy's flying boats out of the water when their hulls needed repair.

There were a lot of cumshaw uses for pontoons, too. A pontoon carried on a flatbed truck with perforated pipe running from the pontoon across the back of the truck made a fine road sprinkler. Several pontoons mounted on stilts, filled with water and left standing in the sun, provided so-

Pontoons Bridge The Gap

A pontoon dry dock at the Navy's PT-boat base at Tulagi in the Solomon Islands.

lar-heated water for a shower bath. Pontoons on stilts also could be used as storage tanks to fill gasoline or oil trucks.

A pontoon with a door cut in its front and a fire inside made a top-notch grill for anything from pancakes to steak. With the fire underneath the pontoon, it made a good baking oven. Add a lock to the door, and it became a vault for storing the battalion payroll or secret war plans.

Two storm-damaged pontoon strings that were salvaged from the Guadalcanal water front were used to bridge a river. The unusual span made it possible for the Marines to advance across the stream with their heavy equipment.

Probably the most important use for the wonderful boxes, however, was as causeways to bridge the distance between ship and shore.

The workhorse of the amphibious force was—and still is—the LST or landing ship, tank. This is a 335-foot ship that carries tanks, trucks, bulldozers, and other heavy equipment from an advance base to the assault beach where the equipment is landed under enemy fire. The LST has a flat bottom and huge bow doors. When it runs aground on the beach, its bow doors open and a ramp drops out so the equipment can drive ashore under its own power.

The LST was designed for use on beaches that drop off to deep water fairly rapidly. Then the ship's bow will run aground close to dry land while her stern remains afloat. But the first Allied invasion against a European enemy was

Pontoons Bridge The Gap

The propeller shaft of a huge outboard motor points skyward. The shaft is raised because the pontoon barge to which it is attached is floating in shallow water.

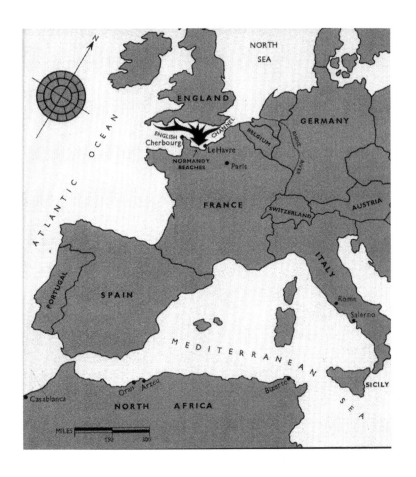

THE EUROPEAN THEATER

to be made on the island of Sicily near the southwest tip of Italy. The best landing beaches there were on the northern coast of the island. They were heavily defended, however, by the German troops that had overrun Italy at Mussolini's invitation. The southern beaches were lightly defended, because the Germans knew that the water was too shallow for American LSTs to reach the beaches. Thousands of American lives could be saved if a way could be found to attack Sicily from the south.

The answer, of course, was to bridge the gap with pontoons.

Up to that time the longest pontoon causeways to be used successfully had been only about 100 feet long. To use the southern invasion beaches, the Allies would need a 300-foot causeway that could be transported across the Mediterranean quickly and installed under fire in unpredictable weather. Navy engineers, however, were sure that a causeway of such dimensions could not be floated across the open sea. The action of the waves would bend and probably break up any pontoon string that long.

Laycock and his engineers in Washington and at Quonset Point attacked the problem from a different angle. It was necessary that the causeway be 300 feet long when it was installed at the landing beach. But there was no reason it had to be that long while it was being transported to the battle area. Perhaps a rig could be devised to telescope a long

A huge crane, mounted on a pontoon barge, is hoisting a pontoon causeway into place for carrying on the side of an LST.

causeway for the trip across the sea and then extend it, like a fireman's ladder, when the full length was needed.

Working against time, they designed new "jewelry" that would make it possible to build a sturdy string of pontoons, 2 pontoons wide and 175 feet long. Two of these strings could be carried by an LST, one slung over each side of the ship above the waterline. In that position they would be safe from the bending action of the waves. When the LST neared the beach, it could drop them into the water. Then Seabee crews would connect them side by side, extending one ahead of the other if a total length of more than 175 feet were needed. If enough overlap were maintained to make sure that the causeway would not bend or pull apart, it would be possible to reach 325 feet, just 25 feet more than the Navy expected to need at Sicily.

Shipment of the units began at once. Soon Seabees and LST skippers were practicing landing the pontoon causeways in secret at Arzeu, on the North African coast. It took about a half hour—less time than that in good weather—for the Seabees to chop the cables, dropping the causeways into the sea, and then rig them for the trip in to shore. When all was ready, the LST would put on full power and head for the beach. The instant the ship's bow touched the bottom, the Seabees would cast off the towline. The causeways, which drew less than two feet of water, would sail on past the ship, almost up to dry land. As soon as the forward section of the two causeways touched the bottom, the other section would be pulled back to the waiting bow ramp of the LST. Minutes after the ship grounded 300 feet from shore, trucks and tanks would be driving over the causeway headed for dry land.

The Seabees' pontoon causeways took the enemy by surprise at Sicily, and they bridged the gap to many another landing before World War II came to an end. The Seabee pontoon units—two officers and about thirty-five men for each causeway—had one of the toughest, wettest, coldest, most unprotected jobs of the war. They rode face down on the causeways as they floated in toward the beach, exposed to bombs, gunfire, floating mines and heavy seas.

The pontoon Seabees had plenty of opportunities to be heroes. At Sicily four Seabees from a pontoon unit—together with an Army man—rescued ninety men from the flaming sea after an LST loaded with gasoline and ammunition blew up. Chief Carpenter's Mate Albert Unkenholz even dived into the water, in spite of burning gasoline and fuel oil, to tie a line on a badly burned soldier.

At Peleliu in the Pacific the Japanese floated mines with the current in an attempt to blow up the causeways. Seabees waded out into the sea and removed the detonators before the mines could do any damage.

When the Allies landed at Salerno, Italy, an American paratrooper who had just floated down from the sky asked who was handling those causeways he had seen down on the beach.

"Oh, they're Seabees," he was told.

The paratrooper shook his head. "And here I thought *we* were the biggest fools in this war!"

5. Can Do At Cactus

THE PILOT GUNNED HIS ENGINES and the big twin-engined amphibian surged forward, slamming Seabee Lieutenant Commander Paul Blundon hard against the stock of the .50-caliber machine gun. From his seat in one of the flying boat's side turrets, Blundon could see the blue water turn to white foam as the plane skimmed across the harbor. Then the sea suddenly turned blue again and began to drop away as the plane's hull left the surface and began its slow climb.

Down below, the temporary camp of the 6th Naval Construction Battalion began to get smaller. Lieutenant Mark Jordan, executive officer of the battalion, who had been standing on the beach waving, became a black speck on the white sand. Then he disappeared into a crowd of other specks, and soon the beach was too far away to pick out the specks at all.

Blundon, officer in charge of the 6th Battalion, watched the Pacific island of Espiritu Santo disappear in the distance. Then he looked at the gun in front of him. He had never fired a .50-caliber machine gun before. He wondered how he would make out as a gunner if the awkward PBY were jumped by a couple of Japanese Zeros. The pilot seemed to be wondering the same thing, for he kept the plane down low, only a hundred feet or so above the water. At this low altitude it would be hard to see from above and even harder to attack. He knew the route from the American base at Espiritu Santo to Guadalcanal in the Solomon Islands Group. And he knew that his big, slow-flying boat would be an easy target for any Japanese fighter planes on the prowl

The Japanese had landed on Guadalcanal in May, 1942, seizing the island from the British. They had built an airstrip at Lunga Point on the northern side of the island, where it threatened the supply line between the United States and Australia. The Allies could not permit this. On August 7 of the same year, the United States Marines landed on Guadalcanal. Two days later they had captured the Japanese airstrip.

Now it was August 20. The enemy still held most of Guadalcanal. The captured Japanese airstrip, which the Marines had named Henderson Field in honor of a Marine aviator killed in the Battle of Midway, was barely usable. But that was where the PBY would land, after first running a gauntlet of ground fire from the embattled Japanese.

For Paul Blundon, Henderson Field was more than just an uncertain destination. It was the reason for his trip. "Cactus," as Guadalcanal was called on the operation orders, was going to be a major base, and the 6th Battalion was to build the mud strip into a first-class airfield.

The plane lumbered in, missing all the snipers' bullets, and came to a bumpy stop. Blundon jumped down into the mud and was greeted by a Marine officer, who took him on a quick tour of the airstrip.

Henderson Field was about three-quarters of a mile long and 150 feet wide. It had been only slightly enlarged by Marine engineers since the Japanese had first hacked it out of the jungle. The Japanese had cleared it, except for a section about the size of two football fields, and had leveled the ground. There was no pavement of any kind, nor was there any system of drainage to carry away the torrential rains that fell nearly every day. The soil was a slippery, spongy muck. Every plane that landed or took off made new ruts in the field. Marine engineers were filling shell holes and trying to smooth the ground for the fighter planes that were landing and taking off at regular intervals. But every day the Marines were losing more planes from accidents on the

The U.S. Marines land at Guadalcanal.

ground than from enemy action. Turning this mud hole into an all-weather field for Marine fighters and Army Air Corps bombers was going to be quite a job for Blundon's Seabees.

Blundon himself had been a civil engineer for twenty-five years. But he had been on active duty in the Navy for only about four months. And even that was a longer period of time than some of the men in his newly formed battalion had served.

Major General A. A. Vandegrift, who later became Commandant of the Marine Corps, was in command of the Marines at Cactus. Blundon told him the Seabees could do the airfield job and recommended that the 6th Battalion be moved to Guadalcanal at once. But the Marines were short of both food and ammunition. They needed the airfield, but they didn't want any more mouths to feed than were absolutely necessary. The General told Blundon to bring just half his battalion. The rest could follow when the American beachhead was wide enough to hold them.

Companies A and D of the 6th Battalion came to Guadalcanal by ship, landing with their equipment at Lunga Point on September 1. That night they dug shallow foxholes in a narrow strip of coconut palm near the airfield and slept on the ground under their ponchos. The next day they took over construction of Henderson Field.

The Seabees immediately began two jobs. The first was

Commander Blundon works at a makeshift desk in his tent on Guadalcanal.

to finish clearing the runway and to lengthen it by nearly a third. The second was to make the surface smooth enough, hard enough and dry enough so that pilots could land and take off without risking their lives or their valuable aircraft. Both jobs had to be done without closing the field to fighter planes. The fighter pilots were flying day and night in support of the Marine ground troops who were doing furious battle only miles away.

The first morning the Seabees were on the job, a lone Japanese bomber dropped a load of bombs near the field, welcoming the 6th Battalion to the war.

But work went on. As one crew cleared new land, another filled ruts and holes in the strip. A third gang of Seabees trucked clay, stone and coral out to the center of the strip. Using this fill, they built up the center higher than the outer edges so that rain would drain off the field. Where the soil was too wet and oozy to pack down, Seabee crews removed about two feet from the surface and replaced it with gravel, coral and clay. In about three weeks the field was ready for surfacing with Marston mat.

Marston mat—also called "pierced plank"—is a metal pavement made of interlocking strips of sheet steel twenty-five feet long and about six inches wide. Each strip is about an eighth of an inch thick. To cut down weight it is perforated like the girders of an Erector set. The strips

(Above) A Seabee driver uses his tractor to uproot a tall palm tree. (Below) Men of the 6th Naval Construction Battalion lay Marston matting on Henderson Field.

are made up into sections about twenty-five feet square, which are joined together with metal pins. Marston mat is easy to transport and it can be laid in any kind of weather. Once it is down it can be used immediately without waiting for anything to dry or harden. Damaged sections can be removed and replaced without delay. It is neither so strong nor so permanent as concrete or blacktop pavement, but there is nothing better for building airstrips in the jungle or roadways in the sand when the rain is pouring down and the enemy is almost at your back.

As soon as the mat was down, the Army Air Corps began bringing in Flying Fortresses, at that time the biggest and best of the American bombers. But construction work at Henderson Field was far from ended.

For several months the Japanese regularly attacked Henderson Field with artillery and naval gunfire. One Japanese gunner, called "Pistol Pete" by the Seabees, kept up a harassing fire from the hills for weeks. Often he destroyed parked planes or tore up sections of Marston mat. A couple of enemy bombers —"Washing Machine Willie" and "Louie the Louse" —came over alone or together at regular intervals.

It took the Seabees a few days to learn to respect the Japanese bombers and artillery. At first the "Bees" took shelter in shallow trenches or shell holes, thinking that any kind of hole was protection enough. But after a few near misses—and one hit by an antipersonnel bomb that killed elev-

Commander Blundon peers out of his foxhole after a Japanese air raid.

en Marines in a shallow gravel pit—they took to building sturdier foxholes. These generally were about four feet deep, three or four feet wide, and as much as nine feet long. Their tops were covered with coconut logs, on which the Seabees piled two or three feet of dirt. These shelters were built near the tents which the Seabees were able to set up after the first few days on the island. With their customary ingenuity, the Seabees took to fixing up their foxholes with sleeping gear, food and such other comforts as they could find.

There is a story that one member of the 14th Battalion, which came to Guadalcanal later in the campaign, dived into his foxhole one day during an air raid only to find that he was face to face with a coiled-up snake. One look and he dived out again, preferring bombs that might miss to a snake that probably wouldn't. At that point a Japanese "daisy cutter"—an anti-personnel bomb that spewed shrapnel and scrap metal in a fifty-foot circle along the surface of the ground—hit near by. That was enough for the Seabee, who sat out the rest of the raid in his foxhole, looking Mr. Snake squarely in the eye!

Air attacks were common and, though often they didn't damage the field much, they always interrupted work. That made the Seabees furious. During one such attack early in October, Seaman Second Class Lawrence "Bucky" Meyer took over a machine gun that was mounted in a pit where he had taken refuge. Later in Washington, Secretary of the

Navy Frank Knox gave Meyer's wife the Silver Star Medal.

The citation that went with the medal described what happened: "Acting unhesitatingly and beyond the call of regular duty, Meyer fired on enemy Zeros during the Japanese strafing attack which followed, and it was observed that tracer bullets from his gun repeatedly struck an enemy plane which was shot down."

Two weeks after this attack, "Bucky" Meyer was killed in action on the Guadalcanal water front. An enemy bomb hit the pontoon barge on which he was moving urgently needed gasoline from a ship to the beach. That was why the medal went to his wife. The citation ended: "He gallantly gave his life in the service of his country."

Shortly after Meyer shot down the Zero, the Japanese opened a fierce counterattack on Henderson Field, pushing the Marine lines back to within 150 feet of the runway. While the Marines dug in and fought back, the Seabees went on working on the field. The Marine lines held, and slowly the Japanese were driven back.

Mid-October was a particularly rough period for the 6th Battalion. Just before noon on the thirteenth, about thirty twin-engine planes attacked Henderson Field. Several direct hits tore up the Marston matting. As Marine fighters took off from the undamaged section of the field, the entire 6th Battalion turned out to repair the runway. Trucks were already standing by with gravel to fill shell or bomb holes.

Seabees pulled out the pins holding the mat sections together and replaced damaged sections with new ones. Other men crawled about the runway picking up bits of shrapnel and pieces of torn matting which might rip an airplane tire. Because there were more men than shovels, some of the Seabees used their helmets to scoop up coral and gravel.

The damage had barely been repaired when the enemy planes returned. They were back twice that afternoon. Each time they left, the Seabees scrambled out of their foxholes to repair the field. The scene was repeated at midnight, but this time it was gunfire from a Japanese naval bombardment that tore up the field.

A fourteen-inch shell from one of the Japanese battleships buried six Seabees in their foxhole near Henderson Field. Howard Osborne and Duncan Gillis, both Shipfitters, First Class, heard the explosion and calls for help. Leaving the safety of their own foxhole, they dug out their buddies in spite of the shell fire exploding all around them. One of the six died before he could be uncovered, but the other five were saved. Osborne and Gillis were awarded the Silver Star for their bravery under fire.

As the naval bombardment ended, three more waves of bombers came over the field. The guns and planes together put twenty-one holes in the Marston mat. The Japanese were determined to put an end to Henderson Field and ground the Marine fighter planes and Army bombers that were spearheading the first American offensive in the Pacific war.

But they had not reckoned with the Seabees. The field was back in operation at 9:30 the next morning, when Japanese planes came back with more bombs. It still was usable after two more attacks during the afternoon and after Japanese cruisers had shelled it for nearly an hour on October 14. That day the Japanese had troop transports standing close by offshore. The Seabees were warned that they might have to help repel an invasion as well as repair the field. Fortunately—perhaps because the Japanese never succeeded in knocking out Henderson Field beyond the Seabees' ability to repair it in jig time—the enemy reinforcements never landed.

During the worst of this three-day attack, the Japanese put fifty-three holes in Henderson Field in forty-eight hours. Although the Seabees kept filling the holes, it seemed safer to move the big Air Corps bombers so that they wouldn't be destroyed on the ground. They were flown to safer fields on the island of Espiritu Santo. These also had been built by the Seabees, of course. But fighters continued to use Henderson. The Seabees still talk about how they kept the field open in spite of the best efforts of the Japanese navy, the Japanese air force, and even Pistol Pete. It was closed to our own bombers for only four hours, and it always was open to our smaller fighter planes.

The big counterattack ended October 17. That day American fighters and anti-aircraft guns knocked down thirty-five out of forty-seven bombers that attacked Henderson Field. From that day on, Japanese bombing and shelling attacks began to taper off. Toward the end of November, the Seabees' work at Henderson Field was finished and they turned the strip over to the Marine engineers.

There were many reasons why the United States won the battle of Guadalcanal. One, of course, was the superb courage of the men of the 1st Marine Division, who bore the brunt of the fighting. But superior equipment and superior skill also paid off. Commander Blundon later compared the mechanical skill and the heavy equipment of his own battalion to the crude tools and large amount of hand labor used by the Japanese on Guadalcanal. He concluded that the Seabees could do in a week what it would take the enemy a month to do. "One Seabee operating a 12-cubic-yard carryall can move as much dirt as 150 Japanese laborers," he said. "At Guadalcanal 100 Seabees could completely repair the damage of a 500-pound bomb hit in 40 minutes, including replacing the steel mat. The same repair job would take the Japanese more than three hours, and they would only have filled the hole with dirt."

Blundon's 6th did a lot of other jobs on Guadalcanal, too. Along the beach they made short ramps out of coconut logs and coral to meet the ramps of landing craft that

Can Do At Cactus

Members of the 4th Special Stevedore Battalion unload drums of gasoline and diesel fuel from a cargo ship onto a pontoon barge at Guadalcanal.

were bringing vehicles and supplies ashore. They also built a number of timber piers, the first of which was destroyed by Pistol Pete the day it was completed.

The 6th built twenty-four miles of road connecting Henderson and the outlying airfields with the harbor. Building roads meant building bridges, too, for there were several rivers between the airfields and the sea. One such span was called the "Mammy Yokum Bridge" because it was such a makeshift job. It was made possible more by Seabee ingenuity and muscle than by following any accepted rules of the construction trade. In order to build another bridge, several Seabees first built a pile driver out of structural steel the Japanese had left behind.

Other men of the 6th took over a Japanese power plant, putting it back into shape to supply electricity for practically all the American facilities on the island. Among its customers were three airstrips with field lights for night operations, the base radio communication station, signal towers, a hospital—built by the Seabees, of course—aviation machine shops, refrigerators for food storage, camp areas and an ice plant. The ice plant also was Japanese, but the Seabees were delighted to take it over. They saw nothing unusual in operating the "Tojo Ice Company" on a tropical island in the middle of a war.

Other Seabee outfits built and fought on Guadalcanal, too, but the 6th had the most difficult time. They were there first. During their early days on the island, they had only two meals a day, because there was no way to get lunch out to the crews working in several different locations. The food wasn't much to brag about anyway. The meat was canned, and the principal vegetable was Japanese rice. There were a few cows on the island plantations, but the Seabees and Marines were not allowed to kill them unless they had already been hit by shellfire.

The cows were so stringy they didn't really add much to the menu. It was a big relief when enough refrigerators were moved to the island to store fresh meat. By November, conditions had improved enough so that the 6th had turkey on both Thanksgiving and Christmas. By Christmas they had built a chapel out of coconut logs and palm thatching. The battalion chaplain said midnight Mass there, and the only bombers heard in the sky that night were American Flying Fortresses.

Early in January Chaplain Gehring held another service, this time to honor the men of the 6th, and the other Americans too, who had died on Guadalcanal. The following day the 6th Battalion boarded a transport and sailed for New Zealand.

The 14th, 18th and 26th Seabees also were at Guadalcanal during the early days. The 14th came in November. They built roads and bridges and also worked on the airfields. They showed their Seabee ingenuity in a number of ways.

Because oxygen was hard to get, they couldn't use their acetylene torches to cut Marston matting. So the 14th built a mechanical cutter using an old V-8 motor they found on a scrap heap, a hydraulic pump from a wrecked bulldozer, and the blade from a broken-down road scraper. To save time on the job of removing torn-up matting from bombed airstrips, one of the 14th Seabees made an old-fashioned plow out of armor plate from a wrecked tank. He hooked it up behind a tractor and tore out twenty-five-foot sections of matting in a few seconds.

The 14th built a bridge over the Nalibiu River, using teak and mahogany, costly woods in the States but plentiful in the jungle. They set up their own sawmill near the groves where they did their logging, and cut 100,000 feet of timber in a month. Laid end to end, that much lumber would make a plank nearly nineteen miles long.

The only troops who could stop the 14th from building roads were our own Marines. The Seabees did their roadwork so close to the front that on one occasion the Marines asked them to stop blasting tree stumps. The concussion from the Seabees' dynamite charges was disturbing the alignment of the Marines' gun emplacements!

The 18th Battalion arrived early in December. Men of the 18th built pontoon barges to unload their equipment, and then went on operating the barges to unload ships in the harbor. They worked on Fighter Strip One, and set a

Seabees of the 14th Battalion use a pile driver and heavy timbers to build a sturdy highway bridge on Guadalcanal.

record for the most Marston mat laid in one day. In that 24-hour period they covered a section of runway 724 feet long and 150 feet wide. The previous record was 600 by 150 feet, which is just the size of two football fields.

Probably the most unusual job at Guadalcanal went to the 26th Seabees. They built the Guadalcanal, Bougainville and Tokyo Railroad, about a mile and a quarter of narrow-gauge track leading inland from a pier terminal. The GB&T RR was built in three days. It was double-tracked for part of its length, and had sidings, twenty-seven switches with spurs leading to supply dumps, and three gasoline-powered engines. The railroad was built to relieve the roads of heavy traffic, and also to test the idea of building small railroads out of prefabricated track sections in spots where rugged terrain or soil conditions made road building a problem.

Only one officer in the 26th had worked on a railroad project before, but that didn't stop the Seabees from doing the job in record time. On August 22, 1943, Lieutenant Commander C. A. Frye, skipper of the 26th, held his own little "golden spike" ceremony. He used a brass spike, which was the best he could get under the circumstances. Then the first train chugged inland at ten miles an hour, its engine pulling a string of under-sized flatcars carrying oil drums. At the end was a red caboose with yellow wheels—actually a flatcar with sides and a couple of benches for the train crew. Guest of honor on the GB&T's maiden run was Captain

William M. Quigley, commander of all naval bases in the Solomon Islands.

Between September, 1942, and the end of the war, seventeen Seabee battalions, five special battalions of cargo handlers, and several Seabee maintenance units served on Guadalcanal. Eventually the island became almost civilized. In fact, by early 1944, Army MP's were patrolling Guadalcanal's highways and giving traffic tickets to the Seabees for driving too fast on their own roads!

History books tell of the bloody fighting between the Japanese army and the United States Marines on Guadalcanal, and of the great naval battles fought off Savo Island, Cape Esperance and Lunga Point. To most historians, the "Battle of Guadalcanal" is a naval engagement in Iron Bottom Bay, which got its name from the large number of ships that were sunk there. But the part played by the Naval Construction Battalions at Guadalcanal is best described in a letter Major General Vandegrift wrote to the "King Bee," Admiral Ben Moreell.

"I do not know how we would have gotten along without the Seabees," he wrote, "and I trust that they will be in every future operation in even larger numbers than at Guadalcanal."

6. Operation Overlord

WHILE THE SEABEES AND MARINES WERE FIGHTING mud, jungle, weather and the Japanese at Guadalcanal, other Navy construction men were fighting another enemy halfway around the world. There were Seabees in North Africa, building bases at Casablanca, Oran, Arzeu and Bizerte. They were at Sicily and Salerno, Italy, too, surprising the Germans and Italians with their new pontoon causeways. And while Seabees were building bases at New Georgia in the Pacific and taking part in the invasions of Bougainville and Tarawa, plans were being made in Washington and London for the biggest invasion of all, Operation Overlord.

The Allies were preparing to cross the stormy English Channel and land huge armies in France, which had been

Operation Overlord

occupied since 1940 by Hitler's German armies. The plan was bold, and carrying it out might well be bloody. But the landing had to be made if the Allies were to free France and win the war in Europe.

Invasion plans were drawn up in great secrecy but, as time went on, the movement of men and supplies across the Atlantic made it plain that D-Day would come in the spring of 1944. Tension mounted as the planners pored over their charts, for Operation Overlord was to be one of the most difficult invasions of all history.

There were two big problems to solve at Normandy, where the Allies intended to land. The first was caused by what the Navy calls the beach gradient, the slope of the land as it rises out of the water. The beaches at Normandy are flat and wide, with shallow sand bars running parallel to the shoreline. Between the bars, the water may be quite deep. The bars themselves change position frequently as storms and tides move the constantly shifting sand. Because the slope of the beaches is very slight, the water moves up the beach as much as a half-mile or more at high tide, only to fall back the same distance about six hours later. As the tide goes out, sea water often is trapped between the bars, forming little streams called "runnels" that flow parallel to the shoreline and pose problems to men and vehicles making their way up the beach.

An LST or other amphibious craft approaching the beach

at Normandy would run aground on a sand bar far out from dry land—even farther from the shore than at Sicily. But vehicles could not simply drive off the ramp and in to the beach, for there would be deep water between the bar and the shore. To make matters worse, if the ships were able to unload at low tide, men and equipment would have to move inshore "on the double" to keep from being overtaken by the tide as it rose again. At high tide, ships would have to unload quickly lest the tide go out, leaving them stranded high and dry, unable to move until the water rose again. Such "dried out" landing craft would be perfect targets for enemy aircraft and shore batteries. Even if they were not hit, they would block traffic on the busy invasion beaches. Once again the Seabees had to devise a way to bridge the wide gap from ship to shore.

The second problem, like the first, was also a matter of geography. The landings were to take place on a tongue of land that juts out into the channel toward England. There would be no sheltered harbors or bays. Since the unloading of men and equipment would take days—or even weeks—some way had to be found to protect the landing beaches from the heavy sea.

The answer to the first problem was the "rhino ferry." This was a pontoon barge thirty boxes long and six wide developed by Captain Laycock and a British naval officer, Captain T. A. Hussey. Other American and British officers

Operation Overlord

LSTs "dried out" on the flat beaches at low tide would be hard to protect from enemy air attack and gunfire.

and enlisted men also worked on the project. The rhino was big enough to carry half the cargo load of an LST. It would be towed to the landing beach and then made fast to the bow ramp of the LST—"married" to it, in Navy lingo. While the LST stood by in deep water, safe from the hazards of Normandy's tides and sand bars, vehicles would be unloaded onto the barge. The barge would then cast off and head for the beach under its own power. Two trips would unload the LST. Then the rhino would move on to a newly arrived LST and start work all over again.

Laycock had an opportunity to describe the rhino idea to Winston Churchill during one of the Prime Minister's visits to Washington. Churchill, who took great interest in anything to do with the Navy, was enthusiastic. So was a group of American and British officers for whom the first rhino ferry was demonstrated at the Advance Base Proving Ground in August 1943.

The rhino got its name from a naval aviator who flew over the proving ground near Quonset Point when the ferry was first being tested. From the air, he said, the thing looked like a huge rhinoceros wallowing in the bay. The two big outboard motors stuck up like an animal's haunches, and the low bow, with its ramp raised up in the air, looked like a rhino's nose with its ugly horn.

The Seabees were given the job of building and operating the rhino ferries. For more than six months men of the

Operation Overlord

A rhino ferry, carrying truckloads of supplies and equipment, heads for the Normandy beach.

81st and 111th Battalions, together with the 1006th Det. which had handled the pontoon causeways at Sicily, labored at several British shipyards. There they formed the long pontoon strings, joined them into barges, mounted motors at one end and installed ramps at the other. Crews from the 81st and 111th, who were to operate the ferries during the invasion, took them to sea in British harbors as fast as they were built and practiced "marrying" them to LSTs.

Meanwhile, Seabee officers, along with United States Army engineers, were working with the British army and navy on a way to protect the landing beaches. What was needed, they decided, was an artificial harbor at each landing beach. It should be big enough to hold about twenty ships at a time, in addition to amphibious craft that would be unloading directly onto the beach. Building such harbors normally would have taken several months. But if the invasion were to succeed, the job would have to be done in less than a week, perhaps even in a day or two. There was only one solution: to build the harbors piece by piece in England, float them across the English Channel, and sink them in place off the coast of France.

The pieces were to be huge concrete floats, each about 200 feet long. They varied in height from twenty-five to sixty feet, the height of a five-story building. The width at the top varied from less than thirty feet to more than fifty feet. The bottoms were two or three times wider than the tops, so that they would remain upright even in heavy seas. The floats were called "phoenixes." They were hollow, of course, so that they would float, and they were equipped with intake valves so that they could be flooded and sunk in place to form the boundaries of the artificial harbors.

D-Day was June 6, 1944.

American troops were to land at two spots on the French coast. The larger, more important landing area was called Omaha Beach. Here eleven rhinos were to be in one of the first assault waves. Later waves brought the total number of rhinos at Omaha to twenty. A few miles west lay Utah Beach, where only eleven rhinos would be needed.

On D-minus-1, the day before the invasion, the Seabees manned their rhinos. Each ferry was taken in tow by an LST, and the invasion fleet headed for France. They made a weird sight—the slow, clumsy-looking LSTs wallowing in the heavy seas, each with a rhino ferry, 300 feet astern, often awash under breaking waves. To complete the picture, a three-by-seven pontoon tug-barge was tacked on the end of a 150-foot towline behind each rhino. But the Seabees, who often envied the "seagoing Navy," were proud to be underway in any kind of craft. As the motley convoy passed the cruiser *Tuscaloosa,* lying at anchor, one of the rhino crewmen hailed the cruiser's bridge:

"Hey, Skipper," he shouted, "how'll you trade your tub for this ship—about even?"

Army troops and vehicles pour out of the mouth of an LST onto the deck of a rhino ferry.

The crossing took all night. It was 5:30 on the morning of D-Day when the rhinos reached the area offshore where they were to marry the LSTs. But the weatherman had obviously not read the operation order. The rhinos were designed to operate in three-foot seas. The swells off Normandy on D-Day were just twice that high, and it took close to two hours to lash the rolling, swaying barges to the more stable ships and to load seventy-five or eighty trucks, tanks, bulldozers and other vehicles on each barge.

There were a good many accidents. The officer in charge of one rhino at Omaha Beach broke his leg. Then a heavy cable snapped, knocking out the chief petty officer who was second in command of the barge. A seaman, George Taiol of the 111th Battalion, suddenly found himself in command of a Navy vessel at sea. He took charge of the crew and completed the marriage. Commander Douglas Jardine, skipper of the 111th, later commended him for "cool and decisive action ... in keeping with the highest traditions of the Naval Service."

The first rhinos to be loaded began moving toward the invasion beaches, under cover of naval gunfire, at about seven o'clock. They had a difficult time making headway in the current and heavy seas. The pontoon tugs helped, and so did small landing craft that were used to give the clumsy barges an extra push or pull, but it was close to noon on D-day before the first barges reached the shore at Omaha Beach. The crews were dead-tired and soaked to the skin. Many of the Army passengers, and perhaps even a few Seabees, were so seasick that any shore—even one held by the enemy—was a welcome sight.

Then came a bitter disappointment.

The Germans had built concrete and steel obstacles along the beach to rip the bottoms out of landing craft. They had anchored mines in the water and buried land mines in the sand. American demolition crews were working at top speed, but they had not finished clearing the beach for the incoming barges. Navy beachmasters, traffic controllers who went ashore with the first wave, signaled the rhinos not to land.

There is a saying in the Navy that there is always someone who doesn't get the word. At Omaha it was Seabee Lieutenant Robert Stilgenbauer, commanding rhino ferry number 10. He didn't see the signal to stand clear, and managed to maneuver his barge between two underwater obstacles. He landed safely on the beach and unloaded his Army tanks and troops. But mines and other obstacles in the water kept him from retracting for several hours. Meanwhile, the tide went out, leaving him stranded several hundred feet from salt water. The ferry sat there, exposed to German shellfire, and maybe a little American ridicule, until the tide rose and floated it again.

But Stilgenbauer and his crew were better off, in spite of the German mortars and 88s, than most of the others. It was the afternoon of D-plus-1 before the beach was cleared for the rest of the rhinos to land. For a full day and a half the Seabees had to man the clumsy, uncomfortable craft against current, wind and sea. And although the LSTs that had towed the rhinos across carried a relief crew for each barge, it was as much as three days before some of the D-day crews actually were relieved.

Conditions were better at Utah. In spite of the weather, four ferries were ashore by midnight on D-day. The rest followed the next day. By the end of D-plus-1, the eleven rhinos at Utah had made a total of sixteen trips to the beach and had landed almost six hundred and fifty vehicles on French soil.

Some of the rhinos struck mines or were hit by shrapnel during the first few days of the landings. Ferry number six at Omaha was struck by shrapnel from an anti-aircraft gun shortly after 11:00 p.m. on D-plus-1. The officer in charge was wounded and lost consciousness. Chief Electrician's Mate Robert M. Miller took over, although he too, along with several other crewmen, had been hit. With only a few of the eighteen-man crew able to carry on, he managed to get the ferry to a ship where the wounded men could be cared for by a Navy doctor.

As the injured were being evacuated, there was another air raid. Chief Miller, who was awarded the Bronze Star for heroism, wasn't ashamed to admit fear. "If you never saw a said later, "you should have seen me!"

Each rhino carried its own bulldozer to pull vehicles and cargo ashore and do all the other jobs that only a bulldozer can do. When rhino number 12 beached for the first time at Omaha in the black of night, its bulldozer rumbled off the ramp and almost immediately hit a mine. Not only was it disabled, but it also blocked the landing ramp so that other equipment couldn't be taken off. Roger Williams, Seabee Shipfitter Second Class, jumped into the water and waded fifty feet to shore. There he found a bulldozer—his citation doesn't say who owned it—and drove back to the barge. First he put a line on the disabled bulldozer and pulled it out of the way. Then he hauled off the rhino's cargo of tanks, ammunition and radio equipment. All the time he was operating the "borrowed" bulldozer, he was in just as much danger of hitting a mine as the first 'dozer had been. But Williams was lucky, as well as being brave.

Several Seabees won commendations at Normandy for saving the lives of soldiers who stepped into deep water after leaving their landing craft. The soldiers, carrying rifles and heavy packs, were nearly helpless in the heavy seas. Constructionman Second Class Laroy Bishop jumped in after a wounded soldier who was in danger of being crushed between the rhino and a landing craft. Without a thought for his own safety, Bishop pulled the man from between the two craft and brought him back aboard the rhino. Another pair of Seabees rescued a soldier whose amphibious "duck" had been hit by a mine. The soldier was unconscious in his sinking vehicle. Other mines in the water around him made it impossible for boats near by to go to his rescue. So Bob Dare and Tom Newman swam through the minefield and dragged the soldier ashore.

The Seabees also had a hand in the dangerous job of clearing obstacles and explosives from the landing beaches. Ensign Lawrence Karnowski, officer in charge of one of the demolition units, became the first Seabee to win the Navy Cross. Karnowski's team was under heavy German fire, but he managed to blast a gap in the line of beach obstacles his unit had been ordered to destroy. He rescued one wounded member of his team and then, after most of his men had been either killed or wounded, he went on to set off charge after charge, finally clearing a safe path to the beach.

While the rhino crews were fighting the seas and the demolition teams were clearing the beaches, other Seabees were crossing the English Channel in some of the strangest craft ever to mount a gun. These were the phoenixes, the concrete floats that were to form the outer harbor at Omaha Beach. Seabee crews had been working offshore, marking with buoys the line on which the phoenix breakwater was to be sunk. They were to complete the job by nightfall on D-plus-1 so that the "mulberry," as the big artificial harbor was to be called, could be built on D-plus-2 as the phoenixes arrived from England.

In spite of the heavy weather, the first phoenixes made their appearance at 10:00 p.m. on D-plus-1. They were eight hours ahead of schedule. They stood offshore overnight, and were maneuvered into position by British tugs the next morning. Then the Seabee riding crews opened the valves to let the sea water rush in to sink the floats. The tugboats held each float in place for the half-hour or so that it took for the big structures to settle on the bottom. Then the Seabees were taken off by boat and the phoenixes were left untended, forming a wall that extended ten feet above the water at high tide and as much as thirty feet above the surface at low water.

It took more than fifty phoenixes to build the mulberry at Omaha, and more than a week of hard work to get all the floats in place. When the last one was sunk, an area of about two square miles was sheltered from the running sea.

In addition to this cove, a smaller harbor was made by sinking a row of old merchant ships. They were manned by merchant seamen and were maneuvered into position the same way the phoenixes were.

Then the crews blew the bottoms out of the old hulls with explosives. The ships settled in about ten feet of water with enough of their hulls above the surface to make a good breakwater. The line of ships—called a "gooseberry" in the secret operation plans—made a fine shelter for small craft

Operation Overlord

(Above) Seabees manned anti-aircraft guns on the phoenixes and rode the ungainly floating concrete breakwaters across the Channel. (Below) An Army tank rolls off the bow ramp of a Seabee rhino ferry at Normandy.

which had to operate between the beach and ships unloading in the artificial harbor. Seabee surveyors worked with the Royal Navy crews that picked the exact spot for the gooseberry and made sure that the ships were sunk in their proper places.

Utah Beach was protected only by a gooseberry. No phoenixes were used there.

Back in England, men of the 108th Construction Battalion had been readying long pontoon causeways to be towed across the Channel. These began to arrive on D-plus-1. They were to be laid in long strips, extending from the high-water mark out beyond the point of the lowest tide at each beach. Then they were to be flooded and sunk in place. Every few hundred feet, a "blister," a platform four pontoons wide and twelve long, would be placed alongside the causeways. As the tide rose and fell on the beach, there always would be a dry section on each causeway. And there always would be a blister to serve as an unloading dock where the water was the right depth for rhinos, tank lighters or other landing craft.

Just as at Sicily, the pontoon causeways at Normandy made it possible for thousands of troops and vehicles to land without getting soaked in the process. Undoubtedly they saved many lives and a great deal of equipment that otherwise would have been lost.

In all, the Seabees assembled 22,806 pontoons for the

Operation Overlord

The "gooseberry" of sunken cargo ships formed a harbor for small craft, served as a mooring pier, and provided some dry shelter for the boat crews.

Normandy invasion, enough of the rugged little boxes to make a single causeway fourteen feet wide and more than ten miles long!

Another device for unloading men and cargo was the spud pier-head. This was a huge pontoon whose weight was partly supported by posts standing on the sandy bottom. The pier-heads were connected to the beach by "whale bridges," eighty-foot spans supported at each end by concrete floats or Seabee pontoon barges. The pier-heads, whale bridges and concrete floats were designed and built by the British, but it was men of the 108th Naval Construction Battalion who rode them across the Channel and installed them at the American beaches in France.

On the morning of June 19, just as the harbor installations seemed nearly complete, a gale descended on the Normandy beaches. For three days, high winds and waves as tall as a two-story building battered the breakwaters and the unprotected areas of the beaches. Small craft were thrown against whale bridges and causeways, wrecking the boats and damaging the harbor installations. Many of the phoenixes were broken up, leaving the inner gooseberry of sunken ships exposed to the heavy seas. The waves caused the bottom of the harbor to shift enough to break the backs of several of the gooseberry ships at both Omaha and Utah. All the rhinos were put out of action. Some of the pontoons were crushed as the barges were thrown against causeways

Operation Overlord

Wrecked landing craft and damaged causeways supply vivid evidence of a violent storm.

or onto the beach. All the outboard motors were damaged. By the fourth day, when the wind began to die down, 286 craft of various sizes, including an LST and 3 freighters, were broached on the beach at Omaha. The situation at Utah was about the same.

If order had not been restored to the beaches at once, the invasion of Normandy might have been a failure. But the Seabees pitched in, along with Army units, to clear the beaches of debris and to salvage boats, barges and other equipment. By June 22, LSTs were unloading directly onto the beach, it being safe then to let them "dry out" between high tides. Seven rhino ferries were back in operation at Omaha that afternoon. The rest were awaiting new engines which were being shipped from England. By the 23rd, the rhinos had begun operating again at Utah.

The mulberry at Omaha was damaged beyond repair. To strengthen the gooseberry, ten more ships were brought to Omaha and sunk alongside those that had withstood the storm. More than twenty new phoenixes were sunk between the old mulberry and the gooseberry to give added protection to the inner harbor. Two causeways at Utah settled so far into the sand during the storm that they had to be taken up and relocated. As the Seabees toiled to repair the damage, the beaches gradually returned to normal. A week after the storm had subsided, more men and vehicles were coming ashore each day than at any time before the gale.

The Seabees stayed in France until the end of the war. They built camps and harbor facilities along the coast and rebuilt the ports of Cherbourg and LeHavre, which had been damaged by German demolition and by Allied bombs and gunfire. One outfit even went to Paris to repair an airfield.

But three Seabee Maintenance Units—the 627th, 628th, and 629th—hold the record for conducting the "seaborne" invasion farthest inland from salt water. They were on hand with small boats, construction equipment and, of course, Captain Laycock's pontoons, when the American forces crossed the Rhine River to plant the American flag on German soil.

7. CONQUEST OF THE MARIANAS

A FEW DAYS BEFORE THE GREAT STORM hit Omaha Beach, a storm of another kind struck with equal fury in the Marianas Islands, 4,000 miles west of Hawaii and less than 2,000 miles from Japan. On June 15, 1944, the 2nd and 4th Marine Divisions landed at Saipan, a twelve-by-five-mile island originally formed by a volcano jutting out of the Pacific Ocean.

The Seabees were in on the fight for Saipan from the very beginning. The 18th and 121st Construction Battalions and small detachments of the 67th and 92nd landed with the Marines. The Seabees handled cargo and kept traffic moving on the assault beaches in spite of heavy fire from the Japanese shore batteries and the rifles of snipers hiding in the jungles.

A good many Seabees who landed that day were wounded. One, Tom Carmody, was hit twice. The first bullet hit his "dog tag"—a metal identification tag worn on a chain around his neck. The thin piece of metal was just strong enough to deflect the bullet, and Carmody got away with a slight flesh wound from a slug that otherwise would have killed him. Later that day, however, he was hit in the elbow by shrapnel from an enemy mortar. This put him out of action for the rest of the battle, but he still was lucky. Many of his mates were wounded more seriously and several were killed.

The Marines had won a solid footing on the island by evening. That night the Seabees slept in a temporary camp ashore. Everyone was a little nervous, including Seaman Don Brubaker of the 121st Battalion. He was on sentry duty at an advance guard post when he heard a noise in the darkness. He challenged the black jungle and heard what sounded like the password. Then he heard more footsteps and the sound of someone moving in the underbrush. He challenged again. This time there was no answer. Brubaker fired. Instantly he heard a body fall and the sound of something thrashing about on the ground. Just then the area was lit up by a star shell fired high overhead by a Japanese gun back in the hills. A few feet away from him, breathing its last snort, Brubaker saw a fatally wounded bull.

The Seabees saw much more than just farm animals on

Over she goes! With propeller raised to prevent damage when it hits the water, a pontoon barge is skidded over the side of an LST at Saipan.

Saipan, however. Most of them saw the front lines, and went a good distance beyond. A few days after D-day, one group was given the job of marking the boundaries of "safe" areas that had been seized from the enemy. As they stood in a clearing driving stakes for marker flags, they were surprised to see a squad of Marines advancing with rifles and flame throwers pointed their way. The Seabees were even more surprised when the Marines told them they were putting up their "safe" markers several hundred yards beyond the Marines' front lines.

On the fourth day of fighting, the Marines captured the Japanese airstrip at a town called Aslito. The 121st Battalion went to work repairing it the next day. Two days later, the first American plane to land on Saipan—a Navy torpedo bomber—touched down on the strip. The entire field, 150 feet wide and nearly a mile long, had been repaired. What was more, the Seabees had widened it by another 200 feet.

The Japanese had operated a small railway between Aslito and Charan Kanoa, a town near the beach where the Marines landed. The railroad was damaged in the fighting, but the Seabees had the roadbed repaired and the engine puffing up the hill again in only four days. Then American bombs, spare parts and aviation gasoline began to flow inland—from what had been a Japanese port to what had been a Japanese airfield, over what had been a Japanese railroad. Aslito became an important field for United States fighters and bombers during the rest of the fight for Saipan.

In spite of fierce Japanese resistance, Saipan was officially secured by July 9. Then the Seabees could turn from assault and emergency repair work to the even bigger task of base development, for the Marianas were to play a key part in the Pacific war.

In the spring of 1944, the Japanese still held the Philippines in a tight grip. They had a powerful base at Truk in the Central Pacific, and were stubbornly resisting American and Australian efforts to drive them out of New Guinea. Guam, Saipan and Tinian, the largest of the Marianas Islands, were vital links in the Japanese supply line to the Southwest Pacific and key outposts in their defense perimeter. Without them, the Japanese could never hold their far-flung empire together. With them, the United States would be another step closer to victory.

After the conquest of Saipan, Guam became the next stop for the American amphibious express. The 3rd Marine Division and the Provisional 1st Marine Brigade hit Guam on July 21. The 25th Construction Battalion landed with the 3rd Marine Division a few miles north of Apra Harbor. The Seabees acted as a shore party for the Marines, moving cargo and equipment across the beaches. The Japanese put up a desperate fight, and for the first few days the Seabees had to man beach defenses as well as handle assault gear.

The 2nd Special Battalion also landed at Guam. The Specials were cargo handling battalions specially recruited from the stevedores and dock crews of America's water fronts. Of course, all the Seabee battalions handled cargo when ships had to be unloaded in a hurry, but the Specials were organized just for that purpose. Their motto was, "Keep the hook moving," and they could unload a ship faster than any other outfits in the world. Since there always was cargo to unload at advance bases, the Specials were welcome wherever they went.

Seabee Maintenance Unit 515 and a small detachment from the 53rd Battalion landed at Guam's southern assault beach with the 1st Provisional Marine Brigade. This was a particularly difficult landing, for the assault boats grounded on a reef several hundred yards offshore. The 53rd Battalion shore party—Seabee Lieutenant F. W. Reeves with less than twenty men—operated waterproof tractors in the shallow water of the reef. They held landing craft steady in the surf while the barges discharged Marine tanks. Then the Seabees led the tanks ashore while enemy gunners in the hills pounded away at tanks and men. Three of the tanks dropped into underwater shell holes on their way in to the beach and were completely submerged. The Seabees were able to haul two of them to safety, in spite of the heavy Japanese artillery barrage.

For five days and nights without relief, five enlisted men from the 53rd operated a crane from a pontoon

Using a bulldozer and man power, a group of Seabees maneuver a pontoon causeway into place during the invasion of Guam.

barge anchored off the reef. Their job was to unload gasoline drums and ammunition from landing barges into amphibious vehicles that could carry such cargo all the way in to shore. Enemy shells dropped all around them and hit one LST close aboard, but the little crane barge and its brave Seabee crew came through safely.

One of the first big jobs at Guam was the development of Apra Harbor, the only good natural harbor on the island. Barely a week after the first landing, the Marines had cleared the Japanese away from the Apra water front and had retaken the Orote Peninsula that overlooks the harbor. The 13th Special Battalion unloaded the first ships to enter the port, while other Seabees went to work building piers and breakwaters. In spite of a storm in late October that destroyed nearly all their work, the Seabees turned Apra into a first-class harbor and built Guam into one of the Navy's most important bases. Eventually it became the advance headquarters of Fleet Admiral Chester Nimitz, Commander in Chief of the United States Pacific Fleet and of the Pacific Ocean Area.

The next target was Tinian, a low, flat island only three miles southwest of Saipan. To conquer it, the Seabees and Marines made one of the oddest—and probably the shortest—invasion crossings of the war.

Saipan and Tinian are only a few miles apart. The invasion of Tinian was to be mounted from Saipan.

To get rock for the giant sea wall built at Apra Harbor, Guam, men of the 76th Battalion blasted nearby cliffs. These two Seabees are using a wagon drill to bore holes for dynamite charges.

Conquest Of The Marianas

During the assault on Tinian, Seabees of the 302nd Battalion operated pontoon barges as floating filling stations to refuel amphibious "alligators" (combination light tank and landing craft.)

Forces would cross the short distance between the two islands and land on the northern coast of Tinian. Unfortunately, however, there were only two good landing beaches at that end of the island. These were heavily defended, for the Japanese now had no place to retreat. They were ready to defend Tinian to the death.

To try to land a major invasion force on these two narrow beaches would be inviting heavy casualties. But the alternative was to scale fifteen-foot coral and limestone cliffs that formed the remainder of the northern coast. Neither the Navy nor the Marine Corps had a vehicle that could do this.

But the Seabees could make one.

Captain Paul Halloran, civil engineer officer on the staff of the task group commander, had an idea. He drew a rough sketch of a Marine amphibious vehicle called an LVT (landing vehicle, tracked). This vehicle, also called an alligator, is a combination light tank and landing craft. Designed to carry the first assault waves of Marines ashore on hostile beaches, it can travel on either water or land.

Along each side of the LVT, Captain Halloran sketched a heavy steel beam about twenty-five feet long, running diagonally up the sides toward the alligator's bow. The tips of the beams extended up and forward like an elephant's tusks. Across the two beams he drew a lattice work of heavy wooden cross-ties like the rungs of a ladder. In his drawing, the crossties at the top of the ladder were bolted to the beams. The rest of the ties were strung on cables. Instead of resting on the steel beams, most of the ties lay across the top of the LVT like a blanket.

Captain Halloran handed the drawing to one of his Seabee officers. Four and a half days later, the Seabees invited him to a demonstration.

The Seabees led Captain Halloran and other senior Navy and Marine Corps staff officers to a point on Saipan's coastline where there were low cliffs just like those at Tinian. There a strange-looking craft was approaching the island across the bay. Its wood-and-steel ramp stuck up in front like a medieval scaling ladder, and that is just what it was.

The LVT grounded in shallow water and crawled toward the cliff on its tank treads. It advanced till the top of the ramp reached the edge of the cliff, where hooks at the top of the ramp caught in the high ground. Then the LVT began to back down. Just then two Seabees jumped from the vehicle and opened the clamps that held the beams of the scaling ladder to its sides. The beams fell free and dug into the sand. As the LVT slowly backed out from under, the flexible part of the ramp fell off the LVT's back and into place on the beams. Then the LVT started forward again and climbed up the ramp onto the high ground.

This was the secret weapon, invented and built by Seabees, that would "widen" the narrow beaches of Tinian. By

(Above) An LVT-2, with ramp raised, approaches White Beach at Tinian. (Below) A scaling ramp from an LVT-2 remains in place on one of Tinian's coral cliffs after the invasion.

placing the scaling ladders on the cliffs on on either side of the assault beaches, the Seabees would make it possible to land many more men and vehicles on the island. These extra troops and tanks could mean the difference between a quick victory and a long, bloody battle.

In the few days remaining before D-day on Tinian, the Seabees and a Marine amphibian tractor outfit built more of the cliff climbers, which promptly were nicknamed "doodlebugs."

On July 24, 1944, the 4th Marine Division, which had rested after its assault on Saipan, made the Tinian landing, along with Seabees from the 18th and 121st Battalions. First a fleet of battleships and cruisers laid a heavy barrage on the well-defended, low-lying beaches. The first assault waves landed while the Japanese were recovering from the bombardment. Then the doodlebugs came out of the sea and started climbing the undefended cliffs. The Japanese, out-smarted and out-flanked, were driven from their beachhead positions.

Tinian fell on August 1. Its loss meant more to Japan than just another hole in a crumbling ring of defenses. For on Tinian, the Seabees of the United States Navy were soon to build the world's largest air base. The conquest put Tokyo within range of American bombers.

8. THE IMPOSSIBLE TAKES LONGER

Building the airfields at Tinian was just about the biggest single job the Seabees undertook during World War II. It involved taking the surface off vast areas of the island and reshaping jungles, mountains and cane fields into the world's largest airdrome. It meant digging out hard mounds of coral and soft pits of loose earth, and then filling ravines and man-made cuts with crushed coral, rock and soil. It meant tearing trees out by the roots, moving millions of tons of earth and coral, blasting with dynamite, cutting and scraping with giant blades, and finishing off the job so carefully that planes could land on the smooth surfaces without difficulty or danger.

Tinian was chosen for the airfields because of its location and shape. The island was twelve miles long and six wide. A fairly flat plateau along its north end offered a good site for several runways. Bases there would put Japan within range of the new B-29 Superfortress bombers that the Army Air Corps was anxious to bring into the Pacific. But the plateau wasn't perfectly level, and it was not quite big enough for the long runways the B-29s would need. The Seabees would still have to cut and fill. And they would have to extend the ends of the long bomber strips more than a thousand feet beyond the end of the naturally high ground.

The Seabees built six big bomber strips at Tinian. Each was about a mile and a half long and about a block wide. The four at what became known as North Field were connected by almost 11 miles of taxiways, with "hardstands" enough to park nearly 300 planes. At West Field a similar network of taxiways, parking and service areas connected two big strips with smaller strips the Seabees built there for the Navy's own use, and with a Japanese strip the Seabees rebuilt for American fighter planes.

To do the huge building job at Tinian, the Navy formed the 6th Construction Brigade. It was made up of two—later three—Construction Regiments. Each regiment contained several battalions. The bulk of the airfield work was done by the 30th Regiment. Roads, fuel storage, housing, waterworks, ammunition dumps and other general construction projects were carried out by the 29th Regiment.

Tinian's shape resembles that of Manhattan, the island on

which New York City is located. The Seabees were quick to see this, especially since Captain Halloran, who now commanded the 6th Brigade, was a New Yorker. Even the early planning charts drawn before the invasion show the island's roads as Broadway, Fifth Avenue and Riverside Drive. Soon the south end became the Battery, and the north became the Bronx. And a bomb depot in the middle even became Central Park.

The Seabees dug and blasted and scraped and hauled more than eleven million cubic yards of earth and coral to build the airstrips on Tinian. That is enough to fill a string of dump trucks parked bumper to bumper in a single line from Washington, D.C. to Kansas City—a distance of more than 900 miles. It would make three Boulder Dams. Piled on a city block, it would form a pyramid about two-thirds of a mile high!

To build an airfield on a strange island requires a lot of planning. This begins with a detailed survey of the area. Normally, this would be done long before the construction forces come ashore. When the site is enemy territory, the invaders have to depend on good maps and photographs. Unfortunately, none of these were available much before the Americans landed on Tinian. There were a few inaccurate Japanese maps, some photographs made by Navy carrier planes and a couple of United States Navy and Marine Corps charts that dated back to the 1930s. From this

The Impossible Takes Longer

A demolition crew places dynamite charges in coral deposits that are too hard to break up with bulldozer blades and power shovels.

sketchy information, Army and Navy planners laid out a rough blueprint for the development of Tinian.

With the capture of Saipan, a few more charts and photographs fell into American hands. And before the Marines set out in their doodlebugs to scale Tinian's cliffs, planes from Navy carriers and from Army fields at Saipan made more flights over the island. They came back with detailed photos. By the time the island was captured, the Seabees knew what they were going to build and approximately how and where they were going to build it.

But this was only the beginning.

Before construction could begin, Seabee surveyors had to scramble over the airfield sites to make detailed measurements. Without this important step, later construction work would turn into wild confusion.

Seabee surveyors often worked under rather difficult circumstances. This certainly was true at Tinian. On one occasion, Captain Halloran and several members of his staff were looking over an airfield site at the north end of the island. "Pop" Shiner, one of the chiefs in the party, noticed a group of Marine tanks with their guns pointed right at the Seabees. Pop and the Captain went over to investigate.

A head popped out of one of the tank hatches. "Who are you?" a voice asked.

"We're Seabees," the Captain answered. "We're going to build an airfield here."

"Well, wait a couple of hours," advised the Marine. "The front line's right here. We haven't taken that ground yet."

Although the island was officially "secured" before most of the airfield work was begun, there still were a good many Japanese soldiers hiding out alone or in small groups. They didn't know they were residents of an American island. Often they sniped at surveying parties with rifles or attacked them with grenades. One surveyor from the 121st Battalion unexpectedly came upon a lone Japanese soldier in a cane field. Before the enemy soldier could pull the pin on his grenade, the Seabee threw a pointed leveling rod—part of his surveying equipment—at him as though it were a harpoon. His quick thinking saved his life.

Other Seabees who did important work before the heavy construction began were the soil engineers. It was their job to decide how much of Tinian's topsoil—called "overburden" by construction men—would have to be scraped off by earth-moving crews and hauled away in order to get down to a firm base for the airstrips.

Tinian, like many Pacific islands, is made largely of coral. This is a hard, shell-like substance formed either by tiny animals called coral polyps or by even tinier plants called coralline algae. Both plant and animal types are formed only under water. Succeeding generations of polyps and growth after growth of algae attach themselves to the top of an extinct volcano or other high spot on the floor of the ocean.

After hundreds or even thousands of years, the coral reef reaches the surface of the water. Changes in the level of the sea or underground shifts that pushed the land up higher have lifted some of these coral formations above water. Such is the case with Guam, Saipan and Tinian. The base of these islands is volcanic rock and hard coral. Mixed in with the topsoil are large coral deposits, some soft and porous, some hard as granite, many quite high above sea level.

To prepare the airstrip sites, the Seabees leveled the ground. They either cut down to a firm coral foundation or poured enough crushed coral onto the ground to make a solid base.

Topsoil was scraped off the sites by Seabees driving huge bulldozers and carryall scrapers. Carryalls, called "pans" by the Seabees, are huge bins that ride on tremendous rubber tires and are pulled by tractors. A scraper blade at the front of the pan picks up loose earth, which is pushed up into the bin by the forward motion of the vehicle. When the pan is full, it is hauled to another location. There its load can be spread evenly or just dumped. To save hauling, good engineers plan their cuts and fills at the same time so that what is dug at one site can be used as fill at another site nearby. The Seabees used 160 pans at Tinian. Without careful planning, they would have needed many more.

The airstrip sites contained many hard, deep coral deposits that had to be cut down to make a uniform foundation. These coral "heads" were attacked with rooters, giant plows weighing as much as 12,000 pounds each. Sometimes they had to be blasted with dynamite. Where there wasn't enough coral to fill in the low spots, the Seabees dug or blasted it out of other nearby deposits and trucked it to the construction sites. Some of the cuts the earth movers made in leveling the sites were as much as fifteen feet deep. In other spots the ground had to be built up as high as a four-story building. Some of these deep fills needed to carry the airstrips over ravines and off the ends of the plateau—were more than a block wide and four blocks long. Digging and moving the coral and earth kept all available power shovels and 220 dump trucks busy 20 hours a day.

Crews and equipment worked in ten-hour shifts. This meant that the construction equipment was in use for twenty hours straight. Then maintenance crews took over for four hours, lubricating and repairing the gear to keep it on the line. Hard, scratchy coral got into everything and wore out equipment fast. Control cables on pans and bulldozers broke from the strain of holding blades against solid coral. Teeth broke off power shovels. Gear boxes were ruined by coral dust. Mufflers and tail pipes rusted and fell off the trucks. Cutting edges of scrapers were bent out of shape. Tires and even shoe soles wore out on the rough, sandpaper surface of the coral pits.

But the work had to be done. Twenty-four welding crews

worked around the clock repairing bulldozers, shovels and pans. The Marines say that the Seabees' favorite supply depot is the nearest junkyard. This certainly was true at Tinian. Shovel teeth were made out of Japanese tank armor; truck mufflers were made from worn-out bazookas that had been discarded by the Marines. One battalion even designed a machine—a sort of cookie cutter connected to a truck jack—to cut shoe soles and heels out of worn-out truck tires. And to cut down the wear on tires, someone got the idea of splicing a circular loop of wire cable on the axles between the dual rear wheels of heavy trucks. Before this was done, chunks of sharp coral often stuck between the tires, cutting the side walls and causing blowouts. But the wire cable, whipping around the wheels, knocked the pieces of coral loose and added thousands of miles to tire life.

The Seabees used an average of 12 tons of dynamite and 4,800 dynamite caps each day to break up hard coral deposits on the airstrip sites or in pits where the material was being dug for fill. It took ninety-five drill rigs to bore holes for the dynamite charges. When all the drills were busy, one Seabee gang talked a Marine tank team into parking in a coral pit and shooting armor-piercing shells into the side of the hill to bore holes for dynamite charges. The idea worked, and someone even figured out that this was cheaper than wearing out drill bits on the tough coral.

As the trucks and pans spread coral on the fields, they were followed by rubber-tired tractors hauling huge "sheepsfoot" rollers. A sheepsfoot is a heavy roller with large cleats

The Impossible Takes Longer

(Above) Sheepsfoot rollers pack down soil for a Pacific island bomber strip. (Below) A 107th Battalion patrol scraper smooths out a road to one of the B-29 bases on Tinian.

or spikes all over its surface. The spikes leave a pattern on the ground like the foot prints of a herd of sheep. As the sheepsfoot is rolled over loose material, the cleats dig into the soil and tamp it down hard. Where a smooth roller would pack down the top layer and leave loose material underneath, the sheepsfoot works down into the material and makes it compact from the bottom up. After a site has been rolled two or three times, the sheepsfoot has done its job. Instead of digging in, it is riding high on a solid surface. Then the pans come by and spread another layer, and the sheepsfoot rollers go to work again. The fills at Tinian were made in layers eight to twelve inches deep. Each layer was tamped down to between six and nine inches by the big rollers. The hard coral topping was eighteen to twenty-four inches thick.

The Marianas have a tropical climate. Heavy rains are common. This was one reason the Seabees had to prepare the airfield sites so carefully. Layers of clay or decayed plant matter under the coral strips might wash away or turn mushy in a heavy rain.

That would cause the surface to cave in under the weight of the big bombers.

To make sure the rain would drain off, the airstrips were made with a slight crown, just as city streets are higher in the middle than at the gutters. The center of a strip 500 feet wide might be built up almost 4 feet higher than the edges. Lengthwise the elevation could not vary more than one foot for every hundred feet of runway. Careful control of elevation required exact surveying and precise filling, rolling and scraping. An uneven spot in one of the runways could mean the loss of a plane and its crew.

Pans were used to dig drainage ditches along the edges to carry water away from the airstrips and taxi-ways. Here again, although tons of earth were moved, the work had to be measured to the inch. For water won't run uphill, even in wartime, and drainage ditches are meant to carry water away, not collect it.

The surface of the airstrips was made of finely crushed coral, rolled with heavy rollers of the smooth-surfaced type used on city streets. Finishing work was done by rubber-tired scrapers called "patrol graders." At this stage no tracked vehicles could drive on the strips. Sprinkler trucks, often made by putting a standard pontoon on a truck and attaching a piece of perforated pipe across the back, dampened the surface to help the tightly packed coral set. As the water wagons dampened the surface, and the patrols honed it with their sharp blades, the coral took on a finish like hard concrete. After a few days of rolling, sprinkling and grading, the strip was ready to receive the heavy B-29s.

There was excitement for the Seabees at Tinian as well as hard work. During the first few months the construction crews often were attacked by Japanese aircraft. Later on, when the first B-29 strips were in use, Seabees working on nearby runways often saw a crippled plane, returning from a mission over Japan, crash and burst into flames on landing. Many a construction man leapt from his bulldozer and ran to rescue trapped or injured airmen from the burning wreckage.

Taxiways and hardstands didn't have to be quite as tough as the airstrips, because they didn't get such rough use. But they had to support the weight of the heavy planes, and the need for planning, careful workmanship and speed in construction was just as great. Hardstands were built at least 500 feet from the airstrips, so that parked planes would not be damaged if there were an accident on the strip. To protect the planes against damage from air raids, the hardstands were placed almost a full city block apart. This meant that a fantastic network of taxiways had to be built at each strip.

There were 15,000 Seabees at Tinian. They drove 570 dump trucks and 200 cargo trucks, 173 pans, 160 tractors and bulldozers and 60 patrol graders while working on the airstrips and other construction jobs on the island. They operated 80 power shovels, a dozen 12-ton rooters, 48 rollers, 90 drills, 5 well-digging rigs, 40 water wagons, 70 welders, and assorted cranes and other pieces of heavy equipment. They built 4 runways at North Field, each more than a mile and a half long, together with 11 miles of taxiways, 265 hardstands, 2 service areas, 173 Quonset huts and 92 other buildings. At West Field the Seabees built a pair of mile-and-a-half runways and 2 shorter strips, with nearly 18 miles of taxiways, 4 service aprons, 361 hardstands and more than 675 buildings.

Every one of the Tinian strips was finished on time. Some were ready ahead of schedule. None took more than fifty-three days to build, except for West Field's Strip Number 2. That one took seventy-three days, but midway in the job plans were changed and the size of the strip was doubled.

As the B-29s began to arrive at Tinian, the Seabees took special pride in the work they had done. The huge, silver planes were hitting directly at the enemy. And the construction men knew this was possible only because the Seabees had been there first. The sight meant a lot to the Seabees, who so often didn't stay around to see their airstrips and advance bases actually put to use. Generally, when the work day went down to nine hours, and the work week went down to six days, it was time for the rugged Seabees to move on to a new island. But there was so much work to be done at Tinian that the Seabees were still there—and still working night and day—when the B-29s started using North Field.

The Seabee outfits that stayed on Tinian to maintain the strips took to adopting individual bomber crews. The airmen soon learned that a crew who named their plane for a Seabee unit was doing the smart thing. Almost as soon as a Seabee painter had finished painting a nickname on the plane, Seabee ice cream, better Quonset huts, washing ma-

(Above) Seabee dump trucks at work on Tinian deposit their loads. (Below) North Field with its three long runways, parking areas, service aprons, quarters for the pilots, and roadways.

chines, better mattresses and all the comforts the Seabees could build or "borrow" began to show up at the airfield. When the crew was out on a mission, off-duty Seabees would hang around the field "sweating out" its safe return. The crews didn't all get back, but those who did were well fixed with Seabee cumshaw for the rest of the war.

As time went on, asphalt plants were set up on the island and the Seabees began covering the porous coral strips with waterproof blacktop. By the end of the war they had laid enough coral paving to make a two-lane road from New York to Cleveland and enough blacktop to pave another from Boston to the White House.

In less than a year, the Seabees changed Tinian from a land of jungle and sugar cane, coral and clay, into the world's biggest airport. It had more runways and more taxiways, and could handle more planes, than New York's La Guardia Field, which was then under construction. And La Guardia was not to be finished for two more years.

The Seabees have many mottoes. Their official one is, "Construimus, Batuimus." This is Latin for, "We build, we fight!" Give a Seabee a tough job and he will probably just answer, "Can do." But the job at Tinian is best described by a sign that hangs in many a Construction Battalion's office:

"The difficult we do immediately. . . . The impossible takes a little longer."

The Seabees in World War II

9. THE BLACK SANDS OF IWO

A NATURAL FOLLOW-UP TO THE MARIANAS was the conquest of Iwo Jima. This pork-chop-shaped island of volcanic rock and steaming, sulphurous black sand lies halfway between Saipan and the home islands of Japan. Iwo is five miles long and about two and a half miles wide at its broadest point. Mount Suribachi, the barren peak on which the Marines raised Old Glory—on a makeshift flagpole put together by a Seabee—dominates its southern end. The rest of the island is a fairly flat plateau. There Seabees and Marines fought and died together in one of the bloodiest campaigns of World War II.

D-Day at Iwo was February 19, 1945. The landing was a difficult one, and the fighting that followed was as savage as in any battle of the war.

There was no sheltered harbor at Iwo, and the seas were rough. Pontoon barges were nearly useless in the assault. One 3 x 12 barge was adrift for more than 40 hours, its engine broken down most of the time. As the barge drifted out to sea, its crew nearly got into a midnight shouting match with an American battleship lying offshore. The barge was drifting helplessly toward the battlewagon when a voice came from the huge ship's bridge:

"Stand off or we'll fire!"

"Don't shoot!" yelled the officer on the barge. "We're American Seabees."

There was a pause. Then came the reply from the battleship. "If you're Seabees, what are you doing out here?"

"That's what we want to know!" answered the Seabee officer.

That was good enough for the captain of the battleship. Convinced that he wasn't being attacked by a Japanese suicide boat, he trained his guns back toward the shore. Meanwhile the Seabees, who had had their fill of war on the high seas, got their outboard motor started and headed back for shore.

On the heavily defended beach, Seabees and Marines were fighting both the Japanese and the slippery sand.

The Japanese had bored into Iwo's rock base to make miles and miles of underground tunnels. When the Navy's big guns bombarded the island, the enemy simply retreated underground. But as the Marines landed, the ships had to stop their heavy shore bombardment. They still could fire at targets inland, but they could no longer let go with everything they had at the beach itself. As the bombardment let up, the Japanese began to come out of their caves to train their guns and mortars on the landing beaches.

Seabees began hitting the beach approximately twenty minutes after the assault began. Their first job was to act as a shore party for the Marines, carrying supplies and ammunition from the water's edge to wherever the Marines happened to be fighting. At first this was on the beach itself, where the Marines and Seabees, pinned down by the withering fire, were trying to dig foxholes in the loose volcanic sand. Later the shore parties carried supplies far inland as the assault troops pushed ahead.

Digging foxholes in the sand was almost impossible. As soon as a hole was a few inches deep, the sides would collapse and the hole would disappear. One of the first Seabees ashore said later, "You just worked your body into the ground."

One group of Seabees landed on the beach alongside a Marine with a "K-9 Corps" war dog. The dog watched for a moment as the Seabees clawed at the sand with their bare hands. Then the fierce animal began to dig alongside one of the Seabees as fast as he could. In a minute, Seabee and

Marine trucks and jeeps sank up to their hubcaps in the soft sand of Iwo Jima's beaches.

war dog were lying side by side, half covered by the sand, as mortar and artillery shells whistled overhead. With every shell burst they wriggled farther into the sand. Then came the command, "Move up!" and man and dog ran forward into the inferno ahead.

At first bulldozers and tanks were the only vehicles that could move on the beach. Anything with wheels quickly bogged down in the sand. The bulldozers were kept busy pulling trucks and weapon carriers ashore from landing craft and over the beaches to higher ground. The big tractors were favorite targets for Japanese artillery and sniper fire, too. Casualties were heavy. Worst hit among the Seabee units was the 133rd Battalion, which lost a quarter of its men on D-Day. Other Seabee outfits also had many killed and wounded.

Some men were lucky. Seaman Frank Riefle jumped from a landing boat and dived into the sand just as a shell burst near by. A piece of shrapnel knocked a ring off the middle finger of his right hand, but he was only scratched. Chief Carpenter's Mate Fred Farina was hit in the back, but his entrenching shovel slowed up the shell fragment enough so that it just buried itself in his pack. "That shovel saved my life," the Chief said afterward. "I've dragged it over the beach ever since, and I aim to take it back home, varnish it, and hang it over the mantle." Another Seabee, Boatswain's Mate Dean Marshall, was only slightly cut when shrapnel

This view inland toward Mount Suribachi shows how crowded the eastern beaches had become by March, 1945.

ripped through his trousers and barely touched his leg. A few seconds later, a second shell burst tossed a heavy sheath knife into his foxhole and skinned the tip of his nose.

In addition to handling supplies and towing all manner of vehicles through the sand, the Seabees helped care for the wounded on the beach. Later, as their own supplies began to come ashore, they laid Marston mat on the sand, from the water's edge to solid ground, so that trucks could drive ashore under their own power. Some of the shore parties served as perimeter guards, and occasionally they found themselves manning automatic rifles in the front lines. But they had come to Iwo to build airfields.

The Japanese had built two fields on Iwo and were working on a third when the Americans landed. By D-plus-1, the Marines had captured one strip. The Seabees went to work immediately, and light observation planes were able to use the field in a few days. At one point in the battle, Seabees were working on this strip while Marines fought for another less than 1,000 yards away. By March 3, 1945, only twelve days after the first landing, all three fields were in American hands and transports were using the southern field to bring in supplies and evacuate the wounded. The island was officially secured in less than a month, but before that the Iwo airstrips were being used by B-29s returning from raids on Tokyo.

Much of the airfield work was done under fire. "To clear

a still-disputed landing strip," one official communique says, "a volunteer party which included cooks, butchers and bakers crawled on their stomachs to the field and tortuously dragged off armfuls of shrapnel and other debris. During the slow, risky operation, the men crept on and off the strip under a continuous hail of mortar and gunfire. Whenever the fire got too heavy, they flattened out, then moved on again."

In their long war, the Seabees had seen almost every possible kind of construction work. But building roads and airstrips on Iwo was a new experience, even for them. The island had been formed by the eruption of underwater volcanoes, which eventually raised their peaks above the surface of the sea. One of the small craters was known to have erupted in recent years, and there was a good deal of minor volcanic activity close to the surface of the ground. Steam spouted from cracks in the ground, both on the slopes of Suribachi and along the plateau. It rose in clouds when bulldozers cut into the black sand or gray volcanic ash. In many places the ground was warm to the touch, so hot that the 95th Battalion had to build specially designed ammunition storage huts because the floors of the standard huts got too hot for safety. Water pumped from underground sometimes was as hot as 180 degrees—hotter than the warm water in most homes.

The caves and tunnels dug by the Japanese army also

The Black Sands Of Iwo

(Above) Steam rises as a power shovel bites into rock to get fill for airfield sites. (Below) Seabees search for Japanese snipers in one of Iwo's many caves.

posed problems. One was the ever-present danger of snipers who often held out in the caves long after the island command officially surrendered. It was common for a four-man surveying team to be escorted by as many as a dozen extra Seabees, just for protection against snipers. One quick-thinking power-shovel operator swung his bucket around and filled the mouth of two caves in a hurry when snipers' bullets began bouncing off his cab.

Another problem was the possibility of cave-ins when roads or airstrips were built above undiscovered caves. More than once, airstrip paving gave way under the weight of a bomber, only to disclose a complicated tunnel structure underground. Seabees leveling the ground for roads or airstrips frequently found tunnels containing supplies, equipment and sometimes dead Japanese soldiers.

The 31st, 62nd, and 133rd Battalions built the three strips at Iwo. Other battalions built housing for the Army Air Force. Still others improved the harbor. The 23rd Special Battalion provided stevedores to unload ships. The 90th built two big tank farms for aviation gasoline and smaller storage areas for automobile gasoline and Diesel fuel. The Seabees laid pipes out into the sea so that gasoline could be pumped directly from tankers in the harbor to the tank farms ashore. The fuel loop that connected the tank farm to the main airfield could feed eighty Superforts at a time.

The fight for Iwo was brutal. It cost a great many lives.

The Black Sands Of Iwo

At the top of Mount Suribachi, U.S. Marines tie the American flag to a pole hastily fashioned by the Seabees.

But it was a necessary battle. The United States needed the island because her bases in the Marianas were more than 1,500 miles from targets in Japan. This was too far to send fighter escorts with the Superforts, and it was a long way home for a bomber that had been damaged by enemy fighters or anti-aircraft fire. Many a crippled B-29 got safely away from its target and limped halfway home, only to run out of fuel and fall helplessly into the sea. There its crew perished, unless an American submarine could be directed to the scene in time.

But the capture of Iwo Jima changed all that. Now the Americans could use Iwo as a forward operating base for the big bombers and as an emergency landing field and repair base for planes in trouble. The two smaller fields were used by fighters. Because of Iwo, United States bombers at last could have fighter cover at the business end of their long flights to the heart of Japan.

10.
VICTORY IN THE PACIFIC

A FEW MONTHS BEFORE THE ASSAULT ON Iwo, United States forces landed in the Philippine Islands. The small garrisons there had been overrun by the Japanese in the spring of 1942. But in October 1944, the Americans returned.

The first landings were near Tacloban on the coast of Leyte. A few miles north of Tacloban, the islands of Leyte and Samar nearly touch. Further south, they lie far apart, forming a fine, sheltered bay called Leyte Gulf. This was the area American planners had chosen for a major base in the Philippines, and it was into Leyte Gulf that the invasion fleet sailed on October 20, 1944.

A Seabee detachment of 18 officers and 510 men landed

with the Army assault troops that morning. They brought with them 11 sets of pontoon causeways and a number of 3 x 7 self-propelled barges. Their job was to help unload LSTs and cargo ships. They were on the job by H-hour-plus-1.

Seabee luck was good at Leyte. There was little surf in the sheltered harbor and it soon became apparent that LSTs could safely come all the way in to the beach. It would not be necessary to lay the causeways out into the bay. So the Seabees turned their causeways sidewise and laid them parallel to the shoreline. There they made an ideal unloading platform for LSTs and other amphibious craft. In spite of enemy gunfire and air attacks, unloading went quickly, and a good beachhead was in American hands by the evening of D-day.

Other Seabee units were close behind the assault forces. Elements of the 12th Construction Regiment arrived in six LSTs on D-plus-4. Theirs was to be the task of building the wild jungle area into a major American advance base.

The Philippines were beyond the range of United States land-based fighters to the south and east. The Japanese, on the other hand, had more than fifty airstrips within easy range of Tacloban. Gaining and keeping control of the air was going to be an important part of the battle of the Philippines. It would have been possible, of course, for Admiral Halsey's aircraft carriers to have stayed in the neighborhood to control the air, but they had urgent business farther north. A few days after the invasion, they met the Japanese

Victory In The Pacific

Heavy columns of smoke billow skyward as naval guns and carrier based planes hammer the shores of Leyte.

Imperial Fleet in a decisive battle that practically put the Japanese navy out of the war. Meanwhile, someone else had to provide air cover for the Army and the Seabees at Leyte.

Accordingly the Seabees and the Army engineers started building airstrips at once. The 61st Naval Construction Battalion was put to work immediately on a fighter strip for the Army Air Forces at Dulag, a few miles south of Tacloban. Meanwhile, the Army pushed inland to seize the Japanese positions that were threatening American operations along the Gulf.

But Leyte soon proved to be a poor site for major construction. Heavy rains fall there seven months of the year. The ground is soft, and in the long rainy season, it turns into a sea of mud. Drainage is poor. Although the Gulf was an ideal harbor, some other spot would have to be found for airstrips, supply depots, ship repair yards, and the other facilities that go to make up a major base.

The answer lay across the bay. The island of Samar was better suited for construction. There, rock and coral were mixed with the mud. Drainage was better and the soil was more stable. The Seabees built a bomber strip for the Army at the southern tip of the island and a ship repair base on the tiny island of Manicani near by. On adjoining Calicoan a 3,000-bed hospital, a PT-boat base, and a huge supply depot were carved out of the jungle. Headquarters of the sprawling complex was at the ancient Samar town of Guiuan, where Seabees pitched in during their off-duty hours to repair and wire a stone church built by Spanish missionaries in the 1860s.

The Filipinos, who had suffered under the Japanese occupation, welcomed the Americans as liberators. Commander Bradford Bowker, skipper of the 61st Battalion, was mistaken for General Douglas MacArthur when he led a four-man reconnaissance party ashore at Guiuan to survey the site. No other Americans had landed there, and the villagers, who knew that there was fighting forty miles to the north, were sure that the tall, lanky man in khaki was the general who had promised to return. Several thousand Filipinos converged on the little town, waving Philippine and American flags that had been hidden for three years. Their enthusiasm was hardly dampened by the Commander's insistence that he was only a Seabee. The local guerrilla army, which had driven the Japanese into the jungle, took charge of the celebration. It lasted all day and late into the night. There was a dinner for the Americans, and a dance in the local schoolhouse, which was lit for the occasion by oil lamps. The enemy had stripped the building of all its electrical fixtures.

The Japanese welcome, however, was a bit less friendly. Pontoon barges carrying ammunition and aviation gasoline from ship to shore were a favorite target for Japanese artillery and air attacks. One combat report tells of a fierce attack against a string of pontoons being towed into place to serve as a wharf. In spite of the enemy fire, the Seabees had it in place in less than an hour. In another attack, an enemy plane that was shot down as it dived toward the beach hit the water and bounced fifteen feet over the heads of two Seabees riding a barge. Air raid alerts became so frequent during the first few weeks at Leyte that the Seabee proprietor of the tent post office hung out a sign that read, "Open between Air Raids." In two months there were more than 100 enemy air raids on the base being built at Samar.

The most unusual combat action in the Philippine campaign, however, came when a group of Seabees under Lieutenant J. D. Piper repelled a Japanese parachute attack on an airfield they were building. The Seabees manned machine guns and rifles to knock the attackers out of the skies as they floated toward the field. A good many Japanese landed safely, but the Seabees held out against them until Army reinforcements arrived. Together, the soldiers and Seabees killed or captured many Japanese.

Two Construction Brigades and part of a third—more than 32,000 Seabees—served in the Leyte-Samar area in 1944 and 1945. Still other Seabees took part in the capture of other islands in the Philippines and the construction of buildings, roads, bases, docks and airstrips for the Army and Navy. The 119th Battalion built a camp near Manila to house Americans who had been held prisoners there by the Japanese for most of the war. It included living and recre-

Victory In The Pacific

Men of the 61st Naval Construction Battalion buid a storage tank for aviation gasoline on a hill overlooking the airstrip at Samar.

ation buildings for more than 4,000 men, and a small hospital. The prisoners, who had been badly treated by their captors, were able to enjoy a few comforts, thanks to the Seabees, while being readied for the long trip home.

The 24th Regiment built a major naval base at Subic Bay, north of Manila. Years later the Seabees would return to Subic to build a permanent peacetime base for use by the United States Seventh Fleet under a treaty between the United States and the Republic of the Philippines.

It was from Leyte Gulf that many of the American forces staged the last invasion of the war, the assault on Okinawa.

Okinawa lies only 350 miles south of Tokyo in a chain of islands commanding the southern supply route to Japan. As long as it remained in Japanese hands, the few enemy merchantmen that had escaped destruction by American submarines could still bring a trickle of food and raw materials to the home islands. Once the Americans had seized Okinawa, however, Japan would be completely isolated. No ship could hope to reach the capital of that dying empire. And with Okinawa, the United States would gain a major base from which to stage one final blow, the invasion of Japan itself.

The task of capturing Okinawa was given to the United States Tenth Army, along with the Third Amphibious Corps of the United States Marines. Three Naval Construction Brigades, each consisting of about five Seabee Battalions, made up the construction force, which also included a group of Army engineers. Construction boss was Seabee Commodore Andrew G. Bisset, who commanded about 16,000 men.

The assault force sailed from Leyte Gulf on March 27, 1945. Carriers, battleships, cruisers and destroyers went ahead to pound the island with guns and bombs for several days before the landing. Then the LSTs approached the beach, with pontoon causeways hoisted into place at their sides, and the battle was on.

Seabees from the 70th Battalion were there to man the causeways. More than 25 of the 2 x 30 strings were laid between the coral reef and the beach. The 128th Battalion was there, too, with nearly one hundred 3 x 12 barges. The little barges ferried cargo from ship to shore. They also served as ambulances to carry wounded soldiers and Marines out to several LSTs that were used as hospital ships during the fighting. Some of the barges were fitted with cranes. They stood by, alongside pontoon piers or at the edge of the coral reef, to transfer cargo from open boats and barges into amphibious vehicles. Still other Seabee barges were used as warping tugs to haul broken-down barges and landing craft off the invasion beaches so that other craft could beach and unload.

The 58th, 71st and 145th Battalions went ashore on D-day to act as shore parties and to begin the big construction job that lay ahead. There were mines and beach obstacles

(Above) On Okinawa an Army truck rolls across a battered Japanese temporarily repaired by the Seabees with logs and coral fill. (Below) Men from the 7th Battalion assemble a pile driver for use in construction work at Okinawa.

to clear, bridges to build, native roads to widen, and airstrips to repair and rebuild. The first airfield seized from the Japanese on Okinawa was repaired and ready to use on D-plus-3. Others were rebuilt by the Seabees and Army engineers as fast as they were captured.

The Japanese fields, which had been built for fighters and light observation planes, were surfaced with only a thin layer of coral, broken by hand and spread by hundreds of Japanese and Okinawan laborers. Before the American heavy bombers and cargo planes could land on them, the Seabees and engineers had to grade and surface the strips with a twelve-inch layer of crushed coral. But with the heavy machinery that had built hundreds of airstrips around the world since the war began, American construction men could do in a few days what had taken the Japanese several months to do by hand. And the Americans could do it a good deal better.

Seabee surveyors went ahead of the construction troops. More than once they found themselves ahead of the Army and Marines, too, laying out roads, airstrips and supply dumps before the land they were surveying had even been captured.

Construction of permanent base facilities was begun before the island was completely captured from the Japanese. Seabee and Army engineer troop strength swelled to 95,000 men as the rugged little island was converted into an airdrome that could handle as many as 4,000 planes.

The huge construction job at Okinawa was nearly completed when the Japanese surrendered on September 2, 1945. Although the war was over, the Seabees and engineers completed the work then in progress on the island. Meanwhile, other Seabees went north to Japan with the occupation troops. Their job was to repair war damage and prepare bases for the American forces that were to maintain order in the shattered country until civilian government could be restored.

It had been a long war. The Seabees had joined it early and fought all the way. They had a habit of showing up where there was excitement and hard work. More than 150 Naval Construction Battalions, 150 Seabee Maintenance Units, 40 Special Battalions and 125 Seabee Detachments—258,872 officers and men—had bulldozed, blasted, shoveled and scraped the surface of the earth from Alaska to South America and from Borneo to the Rhine.

They had learned to stand up against the williwaw —the howling Alaskan wind that is said to drive the snow up your trouser legs and out your collar—and against the hot Pacific sun. They fought the raging storms that churn up and down the English Channel and the hurricanes that batter the Caribbean. They outlasted Pacific typhoons that tore trees from the ground and hurled buildings through the air, as well as the three-month-long monsoon of the South Pacific, which turns the world's driest, dustiest islands into seas of mud.

The Seabees fought the enemy, too, in every theater of war. In the words of James V. Forrestal, who was Secretary

Victory In The Pacific

The "King Bee," Admiral Moreel (left), chats with a Seabee bulldozer operator while inspecting construction projects on Okinawa.

of the Navy during the last years of World War II: "The Seabees have carried the war in the Pacific on their backs.... They paved the way for the success of every major amphibious invasion." The New York Times called them "the unsung heroes of the steamshovel and the monkey wrench, the men who build victory by sweat."

During the invasion of the Admiralty Islands, a Seabee ditcher dug trenches under fire to provide cover for troops coming ashore. In the Treasury Islands, Seabee Aurelio Tassone silenced a Japanese pillbox forever with the blade of his bulldozer as another Seabee, Lieutenant Charles Turnbull, stood in the open covering him with a carbine.

Chester Perkins, a Seabee machinist's mate attached to a Marine unit, was awarded the Air Medal by the commander of the United States Seventh Fleet for piloting an unarmed reconnaissance plane over enemy-held jungles in the Pacific. An unarmed Seabee bulldozed a path through a Saipan jungle so thick with underbrush that the Marines couldn't penetrate it with their tanks.

The Seabees' war had its lighter side, too. At Midway Island, Navy construction men made a new tail for a cow who had lost hers in battle. An outfit in North Africa set up a production line to make more than 2,000 wooden Mickey Mouse, Donald Duck and Porky Pig toys for other Navy units to give to local children at Christmas. Seabee Maintenance Unit 571 invited everyone on a small Pacific island one morning to be the outfit's guests at movies that night, although there was no theater on the island. Then the Seabees went to work, cleared a palm grove, and built a stage, screen and projection booth. They graded the site into a gentle slope and laid the palm trunks in neat rows for benches. The show started, exactly on schedule, at 7:30 that evening.

Throughout the Pacific, off-duty Seabees manufactured "Japanese" knives, swords, flags and other "battle" souvenirs, as well as "native" jewelry, out of scrap materials and sold them to unsuspecting new arrivals in the war zone.

At a news conference during the Iwo Jima campaign, Admiral Halsey told reporters that the Seabees were constructing three airfields on the island. "And if necessary," he added, "they'll build another island and put four or five airfields there."

"Your ingenuity and fortitude have become a legend in the Naval Service," said Admiral Ernest J. King, Commander in Chief of the United States Fleet.

But perhaps the best description of the Seabees comes from a rugged chief petty officer whose name has been forgotten as the story has been passed from battalion to battalion. "Me tough?" he asks. "I wasn't born—I was quarried!"

When the urgent construction work was finished, Seabees frequently built an open-air theater in their own camp area. Here is one they put up at Guadalcanal.

Victory In The Pacific

11.
PEACETIME SEABEES

Most of the wartime Seabees were experienced construction men who joined the Navy "for the duration and six months." Once the war ended, they were in a hurry to get home to their families and their jobs, to take up civilian life again where they had left it three or four years before. By the spring of 1946, the wartime force of almost a quarter of a million Seabees had dwindled to 20,000 men. The number of battalions and other Seabee units had dropped from more than 350 to about 40.

But the Seabees had done such a wonderful job during the war that the Navy was determined to keep the organization alive. Fortunately, a number of Seabee officers and petty officers were men who had been in service before the war. Most of these men remained in the Navy when the war ended. And a good many younger men—particularly those who had not had time to build careers in civilian life before the war—also stayed on when the Navy gave them the chance. These men, together with those who have enlisted since World War II, make up the Seabees of the peacetime Navy. Backing them up, and ready to build and fight again if their country needs them, is an active Seabee Reserve of more than 10,000 officers and men, many of them veterans of World War II.

The peacetime Seabees have earned their keep. Together with the Fleet Marine Force and the Amphibious Forces of the Atlantic and Pacific Fleets, they have developed new amphibious tactics and new methods of advanced base construction. They have built airstrips, repaired bases, radio stations and other advanced bases for the Navy in Northern Africa and the Far East, on Greenland's frozen tundra and at the South Pole.

And in Korea, the peacetime Seabees also had a taste of war.

It was June 1950 when North Korean troops marched across the 38th Parallel which had divided that Asian peninsula into two countries—one Communist, one free—since World War II. Without warning the Communists were invading the Republic of Korea. Quickly the United Nations—particularly the United States—came to her aid. In less than a month, Seabees were loading bulldozers and pontoons aboard LSTs and cargo ships at San Diego, California.

The Seabees in World War II

Peacetime Seabees practice surveying at the Construction Battalion Training Center, Port Hueneme, California.

On September 15, Amphibious Construction Battalion 1 took part in the bold amphibious landing of United Nations forces at Inchon, a few miles from Seoul, the capital of South Korea.

The Inchon landing was a difficult and dangerous one. The tide in Inchon Harbor rises and falls as much as 30 feet in a few hours. Pontoon causeways were difficult to handle in the rushing tidal currents. Once in place, they had to be anchored securely to withstand the force of tons of sea water trying to carry them onto the beach or pull them out to sea.

Later in the Korean War, the Seabees built an airstrip on an island in an enemy-held harbor. The Communists had captured the city of Wonsan, but had neglected to wrest the island of Yo-do from the small force of South Korean Marines entrenched there. North Korean shore batteries commanded the harbor, which ,was an important shipping center, and regularly bombarded Yo-do, but the North Koreans never actually invaded the island. Apparently they thought its little garrison posed no serious threat to their operations in the harbor and ashore.

Meanwhile, United States Navy carrier planes were attacking Wonsan every day. So were Air Force planes based in South Korea and Japan. The aviator whose plane was hit by anti-aircraft fire over Wonsan had the choice of crash-landing in enemy territory and being taken prisoner, if he lived through the landing, or of ditching his plane at sea and hoping for rescue. Neither choice was very attractive, nor was the third choice of parachuting into enemy territory or the sea.

Then the Seabees landed at Yo-do. In nineteen days they built a 2,400-foot airstrip that ran all the way across the island. They did the job under fire from the Communist batteries across the bay. While they were building, they often had to take time out to fill new shell holes in the runway. On the twentieth day, nine Marine pilots landed their damaged Corsair fighters on the strip. In the year that the Yo-do emergency field was in use, it saved the lives of more than sixty Navy, Air Force and Marine Corps fliers, not to mention at least ten million dollars' worth of airplanes that otherwise would have been lost.

In 1951, while the Korean fighting was at its height, the Seabees began the largest "peacetime" construction job in their history. The assignment: to construct a major base for the United States Seventh Fleet at Cubi Point in the Philippines. Cubi Point forms the southern shore of Subic Bay, a harbor used by the United States Navy since the Spanish-American War and the site of a Seabee base at the end of World War II. But the new base, to be built under an agreement between the United States and the Republic of the Philippines, would dwarf anything ever built there before.

Commander Jim Douglas, officer in charge of the 30th

Naval Construction Regiment, arrived at Cubi in September 1951. A small survey detachment had arrived a few days before. During the next two years the arrival of Mobile Construction Battalions 2, 3, 5, 9, and 11 swelled the force to 3,000 Seabees.

Their job was to cut down a thirteen-story hill that ran nearly to the tip of Cubi Point, and to widen the point itself to accommodate an airstrip more than a mile and a half long. Then they were to build a major base there to serve a carrier task force.

The site for the base was a tropical rain forest, where the plants grew almost as fast as the Seabees could clear them away. The jungle was alive with fifteen-foot pythons, ugly lizards, chattering monkeys, bears, screaming parrots and a hundred kinds of insects, all unfriendly to Seabees. The area was not yet free of Huks, Communist-led guerrilla bands that roamed the Philippine jungles and robbed villages and isolated farmers for several years after World War II. The first crews drove their bulldozers to the construction site over jungle trails made by generations of carabao, a species of water buffalo that roamed wild until the Filipinos turned them into farm animals.

The Seabees cut, filled and blasted their way through the jungle until they had built a road to bring their equipment to the site. Trees in the rain forest were as much as one hundred and fifty feet tall and often had trunks six or eight feet in diameter. Beneath them, under the tangled underbrush, the mud might be three feet deep. A Seabee on a bulldozer was no match for these giants. The blasting crews did most of the logging here.

A native village had to be moved before the base could be built. Mobile Construction Battalion 3 helped the villagers move their few possessions, and it was quite a sight to see Seabees ferrying caribao across Subic Bay, a few at a time, in landing craft.

Then the work began in earnest.

The Seabees worked for five years at Cubi Point. As deadlines grew near, they toiled in three shifts each day, six days a week, in rain, heat, mud, dust and burning sun. MCB 2 cut eighty-five feet off the top of Mt. Maritan so that it wouldn't be in the way of planes coming in to land. More than 200,000 cubic yards of rock and soil came down the side of the mountain. The Seabees used it to fill a swamp. A half-million-gallon water tank, built on the mountaintop toward the end of World War II, was put on skids and pulled down to the water's edge. Then it was floated across the bay and set up on dry land, where the Seabees used it to store asphalt. The asphalt later went to pave the miles of streets and highways the Seabees built in and around the base. More of it was poured onto the top of the airstrip.

Alongside the strip, the Seabees built a first-class naval base with piers, wharves and repair shops, ammunition

Peacetime Seabees

A half-million-gallon tank slides down the slope toward Subic Bay and is shoved into the water by a bulldozer.

dumps, fuel storage, a mine depot and housing for several thousand men. Later they built homes there so that officers and men stationed at the base would be able to live ashore with their families.

When the job at Cubi Point was finished, someone figured out that it added up to twenty million man-hours of Seabee labor, and that more earth was moved there than in the digging of the Panama Canal.

But the peacetime Seabees don't spend all their time in tropical jungles. Some of their most exciting jobs have been in Antarctica, where they have carved landing fields and scientific research bases at the bottom of the world.

The Seabees first went to Antarctica in 1947 with a Navy expedition called Operation Highjump led by Rear Admiral Richard E. Byrd. There were 183 Seabees in the task force of 13 ships and 4,000 men. Byrd's Little America base established in 1939-40 was found buried in the snow. Seabees built a new camp near by, with tents for most of the three hundred Americans who were to spend two months ashore there and a more permanent thirty-five-man camp built of specially insulated Quonset huts. Another Seabee job was the unloading of tons of supplies and equipment for the camp and moving it by tractor and sled across the ice.

Operation Highjump lasted only a few months. The expedition sailed for home before the bitter Antarctic winter fell on Little America. The Seabees returned to Antarctica in

1955, however, and they have been there ever since. During the summer of 1955 a new Seabee outfit called Mobile Construction Battalion (Special) was formed at Davisville, Rhode Island, and trained in cold-weather operations. Detachment A of the Special Battalion—nearly 2,000 men, all of them volunteers—sailed for Antarctica in November to take part in Operation Deep Freeze.

The expedition arrived in December, the beginning of the Antarctic summer. At this time of the year, when it is winter in the north, the sun circles around the Antarctic sky all day without setting. Sometimes the temperature climbs up above freezing. During the southern winter, when it is summer north of the Equator, the sun is never seen in the Antarctic and the temperature drops far below zero.

The Seabees built still another new camp at Little America, and they unloaded enough supplies there so that the little outpost was self-sustaining within a few weeks of their arrival. Across the bay at Ross Island, however, another gang of Seabees ran into trouble.

Most of the solid ground at Antarctica can be reached only by crossing a wide strip of bay ice. Ships tie up alongside the ice shelf, securing their lines to "dead men"—Navy slang for timbers frozen solidly into the ice. Men and cargo are unloaded onto the ice and moved by tractor and sled to solid ground. It was in such an operation that Seabee Richard T. Williams lost his life. The tractor he was driving struck a thin spot on the ice shelf and plunged through into the deep water of McMurdo Sound. Weighted down by his heavy clothing, Williams had no chance to save himself. He was gone from sight before anyone could try to help him.

Miles away, another group of Seabees going ashore at Cape Adair were more fortunate. They were tossed into the icy sea when their whaleboat was swamped, but they made their way safely to shore. There they found shelter in a hut built in 1899 by the British explorer Robert Scott. They warmed themselves over a fire made from coal Scott had left behind more than fifty years before.

The purpose of Operation Deep Freeze was to build permanent scientific outposts at Little America and on the shore overlooking McMurdo Sound. Buildings were constructed on solid ground at McMurdo Station and on a layer of snow and ice hundreds of feet deep at Little America. The Seabees built an airstrip on the ice of McMurdo Sound for use by ski-equipped planes.

More than 160 of the Seabees who went to Antarctica with the first Operation Deep Freeze stayed on the ice when the task force sailed north at the end of the Antarctic summer. Along with other military men and scientists, they spent a lonely winter cut off from the world, making scientific observations and doing the essential housekeeping chores that made the scientific program possible.

One of the most important tasks of the wintering-over

(Above) Seabee tractors clear snow from the sea ice at Mc-Murdo Sound to prepare Williams Field for the 1961-62 Operation Deep Freeze. (Below) A 5,000-pound roller is used to pack down the snow on the runway.

party was completion of the ice landing strip at McMurdo. Rear Admiral George Dufek, commander of Operation Deep Freeze II, planned to fly to Antarctica from New Zealand with an advance party in October 1956, rather than waiting until November or December when ships could reach McMurdo Station. This would be the first time a plane had ever flown to the Antarctic continent. Aircraft used by previous Antarctic explorers had been brought there aboard ship.

The Seabees worked on the ice landing field throughout July in temperatures that often fell to sixty-five degrees or more below zero, trying to pack the powdery snow into a usable runway. Then they took a new tack, bulldozing the top six feet of snow off the ice and flooding the runway with sea water. Just as the 6,000-foot strip was nearing completion, a three-day blizzard destroyed the entire project. It took a lot of "Can Do" to go out into the snow and start the job over again, but the Seabees had a 5,000-foot strip ready on schedule for the Admiral's plane. They had added another thousand feet to the runway by the end of October.

On the last day of that month, Admiral Dufek took off from McMurdo with two Navy pilots and landed in a ski-equipped plane at the South Pole. He was the first explorer ever to land at the Pole. All earlier visitors to the bottom of the world had made their way painfully across the frozen land. Dufek's visit was a brief one, but three weeks later two planes made the trip again, this time carrying eight Seabees and a team of sled dogs. Other planes dropped supplies and building materials by parachute. In all, more than 500 tons of material, including a tractor, floated down from the big cargo planes to land on the ice, sometimes right at the Seabee camp, sometimes several hundred yards away. What the wind scattered, the Seabees had to haul back. A few days after the first landing, more Seabees came in by air, and construction of a permanent camp, South Pole Station, was begun.

The buildings the Seabees built at the South Pole are boxlike huts, made of a special, polar building material—successive layers of wood, glass, wool and aluminum. The buildings are connected by tunnels, so that the men who live there for approximately a year at a time can go from one to the other without venturing out into the howling polar blizzards. This is no mere luxury for the average temperature at the Pole during the summer is about thirty-six degrees below zero. During the winter, the average drops to nearly seventy-five below. The thermometer nosedived to 102 degrees below zero during the first winter that Deep Freeze scientists, including four Seabees, spent at the Pole.

At such times it is next to impossible to do even the simplest work outdoors. The bubble in a surveyor's level freezes solid, in spite of antifreeze. An ordinary screwdriver will shatter like glass under moderate strain. Breath freezes, forming icicles on noses and beards. Even in the summer,

Seabee builders scrape the sides of one of the tunnels cut to connect buildings at the new Byrd Station in Antarctica.

there are only about fifty "working days" outdoors at the South Pole.

The Seabees won the only battle ever fought in Antarctica, a continent the nations of the world have agreed to preserve for peaceful endeavor. In January, 1957, a brave Seabee crew seized a four-acre beachhead from an angry army of 150,000 penguins. American scientists needed the site for a base, so the Seabees fenced in the area. Then they collected the young penguins and eggs in baskets and caught the adults in nets. They resettled the flock a short distance away. As often happens in that inhospitable land, a blizzard struck with full force just as the job was finished. When the raging storm was over, the fence was gone and the penguins once more were in undisputed possession of the area. But the Seabees came back fighting and did the job again. The Navy still holds the territory, and the penguins have made their peace with the Seabees and have settled near by.

Every year the Seabees have made life at the American Antarctic stations a bit more comfortable. Now there are movies and a bowling alley on the ice. In 1962 a nuclear reactor began to provide electric power at McMurdo Station. Eventually there will be several reactors in the Antarctic, providing not only light but heat for the buildings, as well.

Part of the steam from the reactor at McMurdo also will be used in a sea-water distilling plant which will provide the busy base with its first really adequate supply of fresh water. The reactor crew at McMurdo is made up mainly of Seabees who have been specially trained for the job. It takes a lot of skill to operate a nuclear power plant, but it's a good deal more comfortable than tending diesel-powered motor generators and oil-fired heaters. And the change from oil to nuclear power will mean that the Navy will have to haul much less fuel to Antarctica every season, a welcome change for the Seabees who will have that much less cargo to unload across the ice shelf.

More than 2,000 Seabees have left their mark on the frozen continent since 1955. They have built more than two hundred buildings at seven American stations there, and they have plowed and bulldozed runways and even roads in the ice and snow.

Two Seabees also have left their names in the Antarctic. The ice runway at McMurdo Sound was named Williams Field for the Seabee who died there in 1955. And United States scientists named an island in Vincennes Bay for Robert C. McIntyre, Seabee Constructionman, First Class, who spent three seasons on the ice.

The peacetime Seabees are trained for their jobs at Port Hueneme, California, and Davisville, Rhode Island. They are organized in Mobile and Amphibious Construction Battalions, both types led by officers of the Navy's Civil Engineer Corps. The Amphibious Seabees' job is to go ashore with the assault troops, to handle cargo on the beach and

Peacetime Seabees

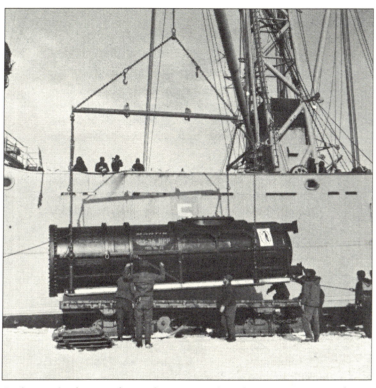

Seabees unload parts of a nuclear power plant from a Navy cargo ship at McMurdo Sound and prepare to carry it by tractor-drawn sled to the construction site.

begin surveying and building as soon as the Marines get a foothold inshore. The Mobile Battalions follow with their heavier equipment to do the major construction work.

Peacetime Seabees have built fuel dumps at Port Lyautey, the Navy's big base in North Africa, and airstrips at Argentia, Newfoundland. American Polaris missile submarines in the North Atlantic are served by a floating dry dock assembled in Scotland by members of MCB 4. Seabees have built housing at Guam and Kwajalein in the Pacific, and at the Navy's Atlantic Fleet base at Guantanamo Bay, Cuba. Other peacetime Seabees have built missile-tracking stations on islands in the Pacific.

In 1955 construction men from ACB One—"Acey Bone" to the Pacific Seabees—bulldozed a training field at the Japanese defense academy in their off-duty hours. (The academy trains officers for all the Japanese armed forces and has American advisors on its staff.) In 1960, when Lake Miragoane in Haiti overflowed its banks and threatened to isolate the southern tip of the island nation, Atlantic Fleet Seabees built a causeway and pontoon bridge and improved several miles of road leading to the isolated area. For the Seabees, the project was good training. For the Haitians, it saved lives and property and was another sign of American to friendship, proof that the United States is a good neighbor.

In some ways the Seabees of the 1960s are much dif-

Peacetime Seabees assembled this floating dock in Scotland to serve the Navy's Polaris missile submarines.

ferent from the Seabees of World War II. Most of the Seabees were men of middle age who learned their construction trades as civilians. They were in the Navy because there was a war. While they gave all they had to the job—and many even gave their lives—most of the wartime Seabees were civilians at heart, eager to get the war behind them and return to their homes.

Today's Seabee is a young man who joined the Navy shortly after he finished school. He went through recruit training with other sailors going to general duty, and he may have served aboard ship as a sailor before being assigned to Seabee training. Once he became a Seabee he was taught a trade by the Navy, either at a school or on the job. The chances are that he spent several months at Port Hueneme. There, in addition to going to classes at the Construction Battalion Training Center, he put in a good many hours learning how to operate heavy construction equipment and how to defend himself in battle. He learned something of the Seabee tradition browsing in the Seabee Museum— which also is open to the public—and listening to stories of World War II and Korea told by some of the older officers and chief petty officers at the Training Center. He found out that being a Seabee means more than just being able to drive a bulldozer or operate a power shovel. He was taught the meaning of the Seabee motto, "We build, we fight!"

Finally, he was ordered to one of the Atlantic or Pacific

Fleet Construction Battalions where he learned to work on a Seabee team, doing any kind of work, any place, under any conditions. As he gained in knowledge and experience, he was advanced in rating. Soon he was wearing a petty officer's "crow" on his sleeve, along with the specialty mark that identifies him as a driver, builder, steelworker, surveyor, or construction electrician. From that day on, he was more than a skilled technician. The Navy had singled him out as a leader of men.

But in one way, today's Seabee is just like the Seabees of World War II. He is ready for any job the Navy wants to give him. Tomorrow he may be ordered to the Arctic or the Antarctic, to cross the Atlantic or to drive a bulldozer on a tropical island in the Pacific or the Caribbean. Perhaps the job will be a peaceful one, building a scientific station or an advance fleet base. Maybe it will be an errand of mercy, helping a community that has been hit by a flood or earthquake. And maybe it won't be so peaceful.

But he's a Seabee, and he knows what his answer will be. Whatever the job, wherever it may be, the Seabees "CAN DO!"

The Seabees in World War II

Bibliography

Bowers, Nathan A.: *The Seabees in the Pacific*, a series of articles in *Engineering News Record*, 1944

Bowman, W. G. et al: *Bulldozers Come First*, McGraw-Hill Publishing Co., 1944

Cave, H. B.: *We Build! We Fight!*, Harper, 1944

Feldt, Cdr. Eric A., RAN: *The Coastwatchers*, Oxford University Press, 1947

Huie, W. B.: *Can Do!*, E. P. Dutton & Co., Inc., 1944

Jordan, Cdr. Mark: *The Can Do Boys at Cactus*, in *Our Navy Magazine*, March 1, 1950

Manning, Rear Adm. J. J.: *The Saga of the Seabees*, in *Think*, May 1947

Moreell, Admiral Ben: *The Seabees in World War II*, in *U. S. Naval Institute Proceedings*, March 1962

Morison, Samuel Eliot: *History of United States Naval Operations in World War II*, Little, Brown & Co., 1947 to 1962 (15 volumes)

Navy Department, Bureau of Yards and Docks: *Building the Navy's Bases in World War II*, U. S. Government Printing Office, 1947 (2 volumes)

——————————— *Civil Engineer Corps Bulletin*, various issues from July, 1947, to April, 1960

——————————— *Seabee News Service*, various issues from Dec. 31, 1943, to July 6, 1945

——————————— Various news releases, newspaper clippings, articles, reports, operation orders, training manuals, technical manuals, letters, and other official records in the Historical Library of the Bureau of Yards and Docks, Washington, D.C.

Stevens, Captain Harry, Jr.: *Polar Construction in the Antarctic*, in the *Military Engineer*, July-August, 1961

INDEX

"Acey Bone," 165, 180, 182
Admiralty Islands, 158
Advance Base Proving Ground, 84
Airport, world's largest, 116, 131
Alaska, 34, 156
Aleutian Islands, 16, 36, 47
"Alligators," 112–113, *illus.* 111
Amphibious Construction Battalions (ACB), 165, 180, 182
Antarctica, 170–180, 183, *illus.* 173, 176, 179
Apra Harbor, 106, 109, *illus.* 110
Arctic, 183
Argentia, Newfoundland, 180
Arthur, Robert, 39–40
Arzeu, 55, 80
Aslito, 105, 106
Australia, 14, 20, 59

B-17 (Flying Fortress), 66, 75
B-29 (Superfortress), 117, 128, 129, 131, 139, 142, 144
Beach gradient, 81
Beachmaster, 90
Bishop, Laroy, 93
Bisset, Andrew G., 153
"Blister," 96
Blundon, Paul, 58–60, 62–63, 72; *illus.* 63, 67
Bobcats, 20–29, 30, 34, 36, *illus.* 23, 24, 27
Borabora, 20–29, 34, 36, *illus.* 23–24, 27
Borneo, 156
Bowker, Bradford, 149
Brubaker, Don, 103
Bureau of Yards and Docks, 16, 42–43
Byrd, Richard E., 170
Byrd Station, *illus.* 176

"Cactus" (Guadalcanal), 60
Calicoan, 148
California, 6, 165, *illus.* 164

"Can Do!" 12, 29, 31, 32, 132, 174, 184
Cape Adair, 172
Cape Esperance, 79
Caribbean, 16, 158, 184
Carmody, Tom, 103
Casualties, 89, 91, 102–103, 137, 142, 144
Caves, on Iwo, 134–135, 140–142, *illus.* 141
Cherbourg, 101
Churchill, Winston, 84
Civil Engineering Corps, 17, 31, 42, 180
"Combat Loading," 20–21, 25
Construction Battalion Training Center, 32, 183, *illus.* 163
Construction Battalions, 17, 34–36, 156, *illus.* 35
  1st CB, 34
  2nd CB, 34
  6th CB, 58–59, 60, 62, 64–65, 69–72, 74–75, *illus.* 65
  7th CB, 154
  14th CB, 68, 75–76, *illus.* 77
  15th CB, 38–39
  18th CB, 75, 76, 78, 102, 115
  25th CB, 106
  26th CB, 75, 78
  31st CB, 142
  47th CB, 4, 9, 11
  53rd CB, 108–109
  58th CB, 155
  61st CB, 148, 149, *illus.* 151
  62nd CB, 142
  70th CB, 153
  71st CB, 155
  76th CB, *illus.* 110
  81st CB, 86
  90th CB, 142
  92nd CB, 102
  95th CB, 140
  107th CB, 125
  108th CB, 96, 98

Index

111th CB, 86, 89
119th CB, 150, 152
121st CB, 102, 103, 105, 115, 121
128th CB, 153
133rd CB, 137, 142
145th CB, 155
302nd CB, 111
Construction Brigade, 36, 117, 150, 153
6th Construction Brigade, 117–118
Construction companies, 34
Construction Regiment, 36, 117
12th Construction Regiment, 146
24th Construction Regiment, 152
29th Construction Regiment, 117
30th Construction Regiment, 117, 167
Coral, 121–122
Coral "heads," 123
Coral reefs, 8, 108
Corsair fighter plane, 166
Cubi Point, 116–170, *illus.* 169
"Cumshaw," 36–41, 50, 74, 75–76, 124, 126, 131, 159, *illus.* 37
Currin, Mike, 5–6, 9

"Daisy cutter," 68
Dare, Bob, 93
Davisville, Rhode Island, 32, 171, 181
Detachments, 156
1006th Detachment, 86
"Doodlebugs" (LVT-2), 115, 120
Douglas, Jim, 167
"Duck," 93
Dufek, George, 174–175
Dulag, 148
Efate, 34
England, 14, 16, 82, 86, 94, 96, 100
English Channel, 80, 82, 86, 94, 96, 98, 158
Espiritu Santo, 38, 59, 71

Farina, Fred, 137
Filipinos, 149, 167–168
Flying Fortress; *see* B-17
France, 14, 22, 80–81, 86, 87, 98, 101
Frye, C. A., 78

Gehring, Chaplain, 75
Germany, 13, 14, 80, 101
Gillis, Duncan, 70
"Gooseberry," 96, 100–101, *illus.* 97
Great Lakes Naval Training Station, 30
Greenland, 163
Guadalcanal, 4, 9, 50, 59–79, 80, *illus.* 61, 63, 65, 73, 77, 160
Guadalcanal, Bougainville and Tokyo Railroad, 78–79
Guam, 14, 106–109, 122, 180, *illus.* 107, 110
Guantanamo Bay, Cuba, 180
Guerrillas, 16, 149, 167

Haiti, 182
Halloran, Paul, 112–113, 118, 120
Halsey, William F., 11–12, 146, 159
Hawaii, 13–14, 20, 102
Henderson Field, 59–60, 62, 64–66, 68–72, 74–76, 78, *illus.* 65
Hickam Field, 13–14
Huks, 167
Hussey, T. A., 82

Iafrate, Frank, 34
Iceland, 14, 17, 34, 36
Inchon Harbor, 165
Italy, 13, 14, 53, 57, 80
Iwo Jima, 133–144, 145, 159, *illus.* 136, 138, 141, 143

Japan, 102, 115, 133, 144, 152, 165
occupation, 156
surrender, 156
Japanese Imperial Fleet, 148
Jardine, Douglas, 89
"Jewelry," 43, 55
Jordan, Mark, 58

Index

"K-9 Corps," 135, 137
Karnowski, Lawrence, 93
Kennedy, Donald, 6
King, Ernest J., 17, 20, 21, 161
"King Bee," 79, *illus.* 157; see also Moreell, Ben
Knox, Frank, 68
Korean War, 163, 165, 166
Kwajalein, 180

Lake Miragoane, 182
Laycock, John, 42–44, 47, 55, 82, 84, 101, *illus.* 44
Le Havre, 101
Leyte, 145–148, 150, *illus.* 147
Leyte Gulf, 145–148, 152, 153, *illus.* 147
Little America, 170–173, *illus.* 173
"Louie the Louse," 66
LST, 9, 50, 53–56, 81–82, 84, 86, 87–93, 98, 100, 109, 146, 153, 163, *illus.* 54, 83, 88, 99, 104 "dried out," 82, 100, *illus.* 83
Lunga Point, 59, 62, 79
LVT, 112–113
LVT-2, 112–115, *illus.* 114

MacArthur, Douglas, 149
McIntyre, Robert C., 180
McMurdo Sound, 172–173, 179, 180, *illus.* 173, 179
McMurdo Station, 172–175, 178, *illus.* 173
Maintenance Units, 156
 515th Maintenance Unit, 108
 571st Maintenance Unit, 159
 627th, 628th, and 629th Maintenance Units, 101
Manicani, 148
Manila, 150, 152
Marianas Islands, 102, 106, 126, 133, 144
Marine Raiders, 5–6, 9
"Marrying" (rhino ferry), 84, 86, 89
Marshall, Dean, 137, 139
Marston mat, 64–66, 69–70, 76, 78, 139, *illus.* 65
Meyer, Lawrence "Bucky," 68–69
Midway Island, 16, 159
Miller, Robert M., 91–92
Mines, 57, 90, 93, *illus.* 119
Minster, Herb, 40-41, 42
Mobile Construction Battalion, 167, 168, 171, 180
Moreell, Ben, *Foreword*, 16–17; 20, 30–31, 79, *illus.* 44, 157
Mottoes, 132
Mount Maritan, 168–169, *illus.* 169
Mount Suribachi, 133, 140, *illus.* 138, 143
Movie theatres (Seabee), 159, *illus.* 160
"Mulberry," 94, 100–101
Munda, 4, 9

New Georgia, 4–11, 80, *illus.* 7, 10
New Guinea, 106
Newman, Tom, 93
Newport, Rhode Island, 17, 20, 21
New Zealand, 6, 14, 20, 38, 75, 174
Nimitz, Chester A., 26, 109
Norfolk, Virginia, 20, 21, 31
Normandy invasion, 81, 84–85, 89, 92, 98, 100, *illus.* 85, 95
North Africa, 16, 32, 55, 80, 163, 180
Nuclear power plant, Antarctica, 178–179, *illus.* 179

Okinawa, 152–156, *illus.* 154, 157
Omaha Beach, 87, 89–92, 94, 98, 100–101, 102
Operation Deep Freeze, 171–177, *illus.* 173, 176
Operation Highjump, 170–171
Operation Overlord, 80–101, *illus.* 83, 85, 88, 95, 97, 99
Orote Peninsula, 109
Osborne, Howard, 70

Painter, Bill, 4–6, 9, 11

Index

"Pans," 122–123
"Patrol graders," 127, *illus.* 125
PBY Flying Boat, 48, 58–60
Pearl Harbor, 13, 17, 43, *illus.* 15
Peleliu, 57
Perkins, Chester, 158
Philippines, 14, 106, 145–152, 166–170, *illus.* 147, 151, 169
"Phoenixes," 87, 94–96, 100–101, *illus.* 95
Piper, J. D., 150
"Pistol Pete," 66, 71, 74
Polaris missile submarines, 180, *illus.* 181
Pontoon, 127, 163, *illus.* 44
  barge, 42, 46, 47, 82, 109, 134, 149–150, *illus.* 51, 54, 73, 76, 104, 111
  bridge, 43, 182
  causeway, 46, 50, 53, 55, 56, 80, 86, 96, 98, 100, 101, 146, 165, 182, *illus.* 54, 99, 107
  crane, 47, *illus.* 54, 109
  dry dock, 48, *illus.* 49
  pier, 46, 153, *illus.* 45
  see also "Rhino ferry"
Port Hueneme, California, 31–32, 180, *illus.* 35, 164
Port Lyautey, 180, 183
PT-Boat base, 48, 148, *illus.* 49

Quigley, William M., 79
Quonset huts, 25
Quonset Point, Rhode Island, 25, 31–32, 34, 55, 84

Railways, 78–79, 105
Reeves, F. W., 108
Rhine River crossing, 101, 156
"Rhino ferry," 82, 84–86, 87–93, 98, 100, 101, *illus.* 85, 88, 95
Riefle, Frank, 137
Rooters, 123
Ross Island, 171–172
Russell Island, 3, 4
Ryan, Robert L., 6, 8–9, 11, *Illus.* 7

Saipan, 102–106, 109, 112, 113, 115, 120, 122, 133, *illus.* 104
Salerno, 57, 80
Samar, 145, 148–151, *illus.* 151
Sand, 135–137, *illus.* 136
Sand bars, 81–82, 84
Scott, Robert, 172
Seabees:
  individual units; *see* Construction Battalions, Construction Brigades, Construction Regiments, Maintenance Units
  mottoes, 132
  name, 34
  organization, 34, 36, 180
  purpose, 16–17
  size, 162–163
  training, 20, 30–34, 182–188, *illus.* 33
Segi Point, 5–11, *illus.* 7, 10
Seoul, Korea, 165
"Sheepsfoot" roller, 126, *illus.* 125
Shiner, "Pop," 120–121
Sicily, 53, 55, 56, 80, 82, 86
Solomon Islands, 40, 59, 79, *illus.* 49
Special Stevedore Battalions, 108–109, 142, 156, *illus.* 73
Spud pier-head, 98
Stevedore Battalions; *see* Special Stevedore Battalions
Stilgenbauer, Robert, 90–91
Straub, Robert C., 38–39
Subic Bay, 152, 166, 168, *illus.* 169
Submarines, 4, 16, 144, 152
Superfortress; *see* B-29
Swanson, Frank, 4–6, 9
Sylvester, Harold McTavish, 20, 22, 26

Tacloban, 145, 146, 148
Taiol, George, 89
Tassone, Aurelio, 158
Temanu, 21
Tides, 8, 81–82, 84, 90–91, 165
Tinian, 106, 109, 112, 113–115,

189

116–132, *illus.* 111, 114, 119, 125
  North Field, 117, 129, 131, *illus.* 130
  West Field, 117, 129
"Tojo Ice Company," 74
Tongatabu, 34
Treasury Islands, 158
Truk, 106
Turnbull, Charles, 158
Tuscaloosa, 87

United Nations, and Korean War, 163, 165
United States Marines, units, 72, 102, 106, 153
Unkenholz, Albert, 56–57
Utah Beach, 87, 91, 96, 98, 100–101

Vaitape, 22
Vandegrift, A. A., 62, 79
Vella Lavella, 40–41, 42
Vincennes Bay (Antarctica), 180

Wake Island, 14
"Washington Machine Willie," 66
"Whale bridges," 98
White Beach, *illus.* 114
Williams, Richard T., 172
Williams, Roger, 92
Williams Field, 180, *illus.* 173
Williwaw, 156
Wonsan, 165

Yards and Docks, Bureau of, 16, 42–43
Yo-do, 165–166

Zeros, Japanese, 59

—Afterword—
BY
Christopher Castillo

I was very honored when Ken Bingham, the gentleman who undertook the task of reprinting *The Seabees of World War II*, asked me to write an afterword for the reprint edition. It really should have been my father, but since he now rests in Arlington Cemetery alongside my mother, it has fallen to me.

My father spent 26 years in the U.S. Navy. His career began during World War II and ended in the midst of the Vietnam War. He had a deep abiding love for the Navy. He was one of the Navy's original 40 public information officers (now known as public affairs officers) and in his last years he was engaged in writing a history of Navy Public Affairs.

I remember driving with him past what was then National Airport outside of Washington, D. C. shortly before he retired. I remarked that the low flying planes passing over the highway made me nervous. He replied, "You should try standing on the island of a carrier during flight ops." There was a pause, and then he said in a slightly sad tone, "I guess I'll never see that again." I remembered those words a few years later, when I was standing on the island of USS COR-

Afterword

AL SEA (CVA-43) off Yankee Station watching the launch and recovery of aircraft engaged in combat operations.

In the mid-1950s, Dad was stationed in Japan at the headquarters of the Commander, Naval Forces, Japan. The Seabee command was located near by. I still remember being fascinated by the statue of the Fighting Bee, holding his tommy-gun and tools, that stood outside that building.

The Seabees of World War II is the second of the children's books that Dad wrote about the U.S. Navy. The first, *All About The U.S. Navy,* written in the early 1960s, is sadly out of date some 50 years later. *The Seabees of World War II* remains somewhat timeless, since it focuses on the accomplishments of this proud organization during the tough fighting that took place in the Pacific during World War II.

The Seabees played a critical role in enabling the United States to win that fight.

As I thought about what to say in this afterword, one of the things that struck me was that the Seabees have carried on the legacy left to this country by those men who stood at that wooden bridge in Concord at the start of the American Revolution. That connection becomes very evident if one thinks of the statue at Concord of the Minuteman with his musket and plow, and the Fighting Bee with his tools and tommy-gun. Both are aspects of the desire to build and the willingness to defend what has been built that have made this country what it is.

In closing, I'd like to thank Ken Bingham and all Seabee volunteers, on behalf of my brother, my sister and myself, for bringing my father's book back into print. Hopefully, it will inspire those who read it to remember, that as Americans, they also share in this proud legacy and that whatever the tasks they face, they also "Can Do".

CHRISTOPHER CASTILLO
Santa Clara, California
August 2010

Made in the USA
Lexington, KY
18 October 2012